Listen for the Wh

Coping with
Learning to L   in

Listen for the Whispers

Coping with Grief and Learning to Live Again

by Kim Kluxen Meredith

CABLE PUBLISHING

Brule, Wisconsin

LISTEN FOR THE WHISPERS

First Edition

Published by:
Cable Publishing
14090 E Keinenen Rd
Brule, WI 54820

Website: cablepublishing.com
E-mail: nan@cablepublishing.com

Hardcover: ISBN 13: 978-1-934980-47-7
            ISBN 10: 1-934980-47-1

Soft cover: ISBN 13: 978-1-934980-48-4
             ISBN 10: 1-934980-48-X

Library of Congress Control Number: 2010928367

Printed in the United States of America

Seeds of Love

To our dear children David, Samantha, and Richard. Our story is a tribute to the abundant love that we continue to share and nurture as a family. Although you can no longer see him, I know that you feel your father's love, strength, and guidance every day. He will always be with you.

And my continuous love goes to Norma and Dave Kluxen. Thank you for sharing your special first son with me. It was in our bountiful garden of love that our precious children blossomed.

TABLE OF CONTENTS

Thoughts on Grieving *by Joy Ufema*

Whispers

Part I—My Story

Section One: The Crisis

Section Two: The Aftermath

Section Three: Details

G is for Grounded. Believe in your "little voice" and let it guide you to your "bigger voice"

R is for Re-building. Start your own construction project

I is for Inspiration. Innocent eyes are watching

E is for Energize. Plug back into life on a different current

F is for Fun. "Laugh often"

Space for twelve months of self-exploration

David Stewart Kluxen Jr.

Loving, supportive husband
Devoted, patient father
Caring and compassionate lawyer
Beloved son and brother

THOUGHTS ON GRIEVING

If the job of the writer is to show up, Kim Kluxen Meredith arrived ready to work. Listening to the "whispers" of the universe, she shares with her readers an experience that could be waiting for each of us.

The problem with grief work is that it's unmapped territory. Even if there were a magic guidebook, survivors are too preoccupied to focus on lengthy tomes.

The bereaved may feel like they're losing their sanity. The desire to reunite with a loved one can be manifested by "seeing" them on a passing bus. It's rough business.

Rituals that once served us well have been diminished to superficiality. Black armbands that told others to be gentle with us were relegated to the attic along with the black wreath to be placed on the front door as a sign of mourning. It reminded rowdy children on bicycles to cease sounding horns and bells...someone inside was sad.

Today, grievers forego attending graveside services to rush back to the office. Mourners at the cemetery take part in a brief blessing, then mingle for a few minutes before driving home to grieve alone. They return to work the next day with a vague sensation of loss and bewilderment.

Death affects us and we get into trouble pretending it does not. Widows do not require a burial site or headstone to visit in order to grieve. They do need, however, to be in agreement with their husbands' final requests.

Readers will find the value of that difficult but honest dialogue throughout this fine book. Eventually, survivors who say "yes" to death then say "yes" to life. But they are not, nor will they ever be, the same. They know, too well, that a life has ended but the relationship with their loved one never will.

—Joy Ufema, RN, MS, Thanatologist and author of
Insights on Death & Dying

Whispers...

Sometimes I hear them. Sometimes I do not. They can be as subtle as the gentle tinkling of the delicate miniature brass wind chime outside my bedroom on a warm summer evening, or as unsettling as the vivid, sweat-inducing dreams that leave me shivering and cold on a lonely winter's night. These are the messages that I believe God has given me as He majestically guides me through the many paths of my complex life journey.

I am not unique. We all have these *whispers*. Some call them the little voices within themselves while others think of them as a feeling, or instinct. Sometimes our daily lives become so cluttered and artificially complicated with minutiae, though, that we fail to acknowledge the simple important signals flashing right in front of us. At other times, perhaps out of fear or a lack of understanding, we consciously choose not to heed our whispers.

The layers of our past and present experiences feather the nest of our future lives, yet sometimes we are unprepared and caught off guard by the sudden loss of a loved one, partner, spouse, or significant other. We feel comfortable and secure while the loving bond is intact, but we can suddenly find ourselves thrashing in a dark sea of pain, loneliness, and self-doubt when it cruelly dissolves.

Although we can neither touch nor see it, grief produces a true physical pain that is palpable and intimidating and demands to be noticed. I have felt this foreign, vivid pain deep within my body and came to understand that its primary source was my untimely loss and deep despair. I experienced awful, debilitating fear that made me wonder if I would ever be able to make a future independent decision or once again feel a peaceful moment of joy.

My whispers guided me down a path of healing and returned me to a state of happiness. I will never be the same person I was before this journey, but I have embraced the new me—and I am getting to know and like her.

I warmly extend my hand to you in hopes that you may learn to *listen for the whispers*...and emerge a little stronger...and stand a little taller.

Part I

My Story

Section One: The Crisis

Section One: The Crisis

Introduction

> *"It is only in sorrow that bad weather masters us; in joy we face the storm and defy it."* —**Amelia Barr**

Relationships come in many packages. A spouse or significant other is also a best friend with whom we share our deepest feelings. Our union gives us a sense of security and peace. We are drawn to this attachment for companionship during our life journey; one's mate acts as a sounding board for life's shouts and provides support for challenging decisions. An intimate partner helps to validate and enhance one's own existence by his or her presence.

Probably the furthest thought from our minds is the utterance of a final goodbye, and it is doubtful that any of us will live unscathed by a loved one's passing. While in the security of a relationship, we intellectually tuck this dreaded notion away in a private, obscure place—like a shameful secret. Then, when that unwelcome lethal summons arrives, our mutually woven fabric is mercilessly torn and we are set adrift. We are confused, cruelly entangled in the emotional shreds of our now-sabotaged relationship.

This shocking severance can occur in many different ways. It may be the final stage of life transported by accident or disease. It may be the unsolicited, irrevocable breaking of a relationship by divorce, abandonment, or indifference—and although the person is still physically there, the emotional void is as powerful as the permanent departure of a loved one.

No matter what the circumstances, we feel powerless and hurt—wanting just to wake up and have the trauma go away and be whole again. We have lost our sense of reality. We want to bring back that person and smile and laugh again. We want to pick up where we left off and return to what was our own normality...and go on forever.

Some of us are totally blindsided by the end of a relationship, and this intensifies our pain. Then there are those of us who are given the gift of time. Sometimes we have days, or weeks, or even months to attend to unfinished business in the twilight of our relationship.

But none of us can really prepare for something that we have never experienced. We cannot plan our farewells. No one really wants to say goodbye.

We would all prefer to have more time.

Grief is the protective state we are forced into while our bodies, minds, and hearts sort out the broken pieces. It is a heavy, dull feeling that forces us to slow down and prepare for healing. It is a cloudy and confusing sense of being that sometimes masks the true self. I think of it as nature's

umbrella—an invisible covering that shields us from further harm and allows healing.

Grief gives us a chance to re-examine what we had and what we lost. It cracks open our hardened outer shell and exposes our fragile inner being, making us feel vulnerable. Our partner...our loved one...our safety net...has suddenly been taken away, leaving fear, loneliness, and a trace of anger to temporarily fill the void. But we have to remember that grief is only a temporary way station in life's journey. We cannot remain in hiding from unknown future loss and more pain. We must eventually move on as best as we can—continuing to live and be lively.

We instinctively cry out for help. For some of us, our pleas may be strong and bellowing, like the shouts of a hiker stranded deep in the woods. Or they may be tentative and meek utterances, like a wounded child's whimper muffled in the cracks of a concrete sidewalk after a fall. But for all of us, these appeals are real, and the manner in which we choose to communicate our need for healing is just as important and unique as the relationships we nurtured and which led to our pain.

The recipe for recovery for each of us is also unique; while we are not able to control our circumstances, we can control our reactions. We can reach out to others who have experienced the power of grief and learn that healing comes with time and that the human spirit is amazingly resilient, even in the face of our darkest and most frightening hour. We can lean on each other and then, in turn, someday perhaps we, too, can provide a steady hand for a new traveler struggling through grief's journey.

A piece of your heart will always belong to the one for whom you grieve. You invested your emotions, you gave of yourself, and that can never be erased.

My personal journey through the grieving process began with a few tentative baby steps that slowly progressed to self-assured strides. I jotted down my thoughts through the years as I slowly healed, and I now share them with you.

Chapter I

The Beginning

"This is the man that you are going to marry!" That whisper transformed me into a wife, mother, and best friend.

My rusty, outdated black Ford LTD sedan cruised down the narrow Delaware County, Pennsylvania, roadway at a steady 50 miles per hour. Dilapidated, whitewashed wooden horse fences protected the pristine pastures from the crumbling asphalt shoulders—their bleached outlines whizzing past my peripheral vision like frames in an old 35-millimeter home movie. Suddenly, a low but insistent voice entered my head. "This is the man that you are going to marry!"

Since my January 1976 graduation from the Institute for Paralegal Training in Philadelphia, I had been working as a commercial litigation paralegal for a Center City law firm. Due to the surplus of high school language teachers in the area, my B.A. degree in Spanish from Washington College in Chestertown, Maryland, did not lead to immediate employment as an educator. As a result, I completely switched gears and ventured into a new area of study, law. Perhaps watching *Perry Mason* on television in my youth and my girlish crush on Mason's assistant, Paul Drake, subconsciously lured me into this new legal world. Otherwise, I have to admit that there was no real rationale for my career switch. I was young, impressionable, and adventurous.

It was fall. Several weeks prior, while going through my bottomless stack of interrogatories, I had noticed a handsome, dark-haired third-year law intern rushing past the door of my tiny inner office. (As a paralegal, I did not merit an office with a window; the corner offices, with 180-degree views of the City of Brotherly Love, were awarded to the sage and experienced senior partners.) An unfiltered cigarette dangled recklessly from his mouth and his thinning fine hair stood up on end. His maroon-and-white polka-dot tie brushed up against the doorjamb, signaling my attention like the checkered flag at an auto race. Suddenly a familiar shout from the head of the trial department echoed from the far end of the hallway. "Coming, Foster!" the intern responded confidently to his boss.

At this particular moment in my life, I was reluctantly near the end of a five-year relationship with my college sweetheart. I was dreading the impending breakup and had retreated safely into denial. Upon graduating from college in May 1974, I was anxious to continue on to the next traditional step, marriage, like so many of my Zeta Tau Alpha sorority sisters had done before me. But matrimony was the furthest thing from my boyfriend's mind. Athletic, fun-loving, and hesitant to commit, he tentatively entered the adult workforce as a banker and remained dedicated to partying

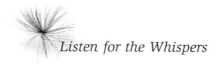

with his lacrosse buddies at night. One day, after a strained silent lunch together at his favorite deli counter in a dim, sub-street-level establishment near the famous Wanamaker's department store, we started arguing at the busy Philadelphia intersection of Broad and Walnut streets—and I could feel our relationship finally unraveling. Our angry words were muffled by the passing traffic; tears welled in my eyes and stung my cheeks as they mixed with the fumes from the noisy city buses. My unrealistic dreams of romantic weekends at the Jersey Shore and carefree days together in the suburbs were fading like the afternoon sun. Knowing deep down that this was the end, I turned and walked back to my office on the other side of City Hall. I pulled my emerald-green wool blazer close to my trembling body. My chest started to hurt. Although broken, my heart continued to pound with anger and sorrow.

Upon my return to work, I noticed that the intern, in his shiny black tasseled loafers, continued to pace up and down the short corridor connecting our offices. Since we both were considered legal support staff, our adjoining workspaces were positioned in the interior section of the building; the entire seventeenth floor was a maze of cubicles and secretarial stations abuzz with electric typewriters and ringing telephones. His navy pinstriped suit was immaculate save for the shiny patches on the elbows and seat indicating overuse. And his attractive, yet unrecognizable, cologne drifted in and pleasantly stirred the stale air of my poorly ventilated cubbyhole. Smells always trigger memories for me; to this day even the hint of a nearby cigar instantly reminds me of my father's upstate New York construction office, which was permanently infused with a blend of cigar smoke, diesel fuel, and his secretary's pungent gardenia perfume.

The intern appeared to have endless energy. In the days that followed my first sighting, my investigative paralegal skills helped me learn that his name was David and he was four years my senior. He was a third-year law student from Villanova University, a part-time intern for the trial division, a Naval Reserve flyer, and a recently divorced father of an adorable four-year-old blond-haired namesake whose picture was proudly displayed in a small silver frame on the corner of his desk. In contrast, I was a rejected single, naïve college graduate with a bruised ego and shattered dreams. His hearty laugh and twinkling eyes captivated and amused me from a distance. At the moment, his presence was only a pleasant distraction from my relentless routine but he would soon become my savior—guiding me back into love like the mighty beacon of a lighthouse on a rocky New England shore.

There were a few opportunities for small talk and a quick smile, and then David and I started lunching together. We both were on limited budgets, so our meals were simple and cheap. Philly cheesesteaks and shrimp salad sandwiches on rye were our mainstays. As the days turned into weeks, our lunches became more frequent, and eventually we graduated to socializing after work. The local 1970s-era

watering holes in Philadelphia were perfect for blaring disco music, cheap fruity drinks, and free salty snacks that often substituted for dinner. Sometimes it was just the two of us, and at other times we were joined by several young male associates from our firm. We all craved a distraction from the drudgery of legal research and mountains of paperwork, and we usually exited the building as a team. Often I was the only skirt in a sea of blue rumpled suits and limp ties. This novel diversion gave me a new sense of confidence; it substituted for the nostalgic raucous atmosphere of college fraternity parties I had left behind.

One night, David and I caught the SEPTA commuter train back to the University of Villanova station together. The near-empty silver cars glided swiftly over the rusty tracks as we opened ourselves ever so slightly to one another. The revelations were carefully measured by each of us so as not to make us too vulnerable; the bruises from his divorce and scars from my breakup were still fresh. With each passing town on the Main Line our personal histories unfolded. Overlook... Ardmore... Bryn Mawr... Cautiously we peered into the windows of each other's soul, yet we remained strangers on this train. On the platform at our destination, we parted with a smile and wave. His late-model, burnt-orange Pinto station wagon laboriously chugged over the wooden train trestle into the night while my oversized black LTD sedan greedily devoured the pavement towards my Newtown Square walk-up.

As much as I anticipated the unveiling of new secrets, I

found it difficult to let go of five years of treasured romantic memories. My future had been spun into them like the intricate pattern of a spider web, and I was afraid of failure. I resisted the temptation to listen to the overpowering message as it echoed in my head—even turning the car radio off for fear that the words would magically, and loudly, be broadcast over the airwaves for the entire world to hear. The *whisper* doggedly remained. It kept repeating, "This is the man that you are going to marry!" "But I don't love him... I hardly even know him!" I blurted aloud, startling myself as I clutched the steering wheel. Even in the privacy of my vehicle, I felt my face redden in embarrassment. David and I were merely office neighbors, for heaven's sake! Why was this ludicrous thought replaying in my mind? Where did it come from and why?

Four months later, on New Year's Eve 1976, David Stewart Kluxen Jr. asked me to marry him in front of the gas stove in my tiny apartment. Nine months later, on Labor Day weekend, September 3, 1977, we were married at 4:00 p.m. in a small, white clapboard Methodist church in Ames, New York.

Chapter II

The Accident

The harsh whisper of the sirens interrupted the silence of the night. It heralded our change from four to three.

David's faded brown 1981 Volvo station wagon lumbered into the left bay of our two-car garage early on the evening of February 10, 1993. Its motor idled anxiously. I glanced at the small digital clock on the kitchen stove; it was 5:40. My husband had forgotten his haircut appointment, I surmised, since he was home unusually early. The side door from our house to the garage was still open from my trip to the end of the driveway for the evening paper. Through the dusty screen door I could barely make out the familiar outline of our car. The engine continued to hum its tired melody in anticipation of its next departure. Its customary echo in the garage did not alert our cairn terrier Harry, who was stretched out in the next room on his back with his legs in the air, asleep.

I went back to slicing up yellow onions and green peppers for our favorite shish kabob dinner. Even though it was winter, I still liked to use the propane grill on the back patio. This winter the snow was unusually late, so I only had to brave the cold temperature.

Still within shouting distance of the screen door, I ribbed, "Are you handsome yet?" David was not one to pay a great deal of attention to his hair; he did not spend the hours and dollars that I did seeking the ideal coif. Instead, he was merely grateful to hang onto as much hair as possible. Tiny nest-like clumps of his brown and gray hair greeted me each morning as I prepared to shower. If only I could recycle these soggy filaments and find a use for them, I mused as every morning as I plucked them from the drain.

Lately David had been looking particularly tired, so I had made a haircut appointment for him with our son's barber. It was not unusual for him to put in twelve-hour days at his two-man law firm seven miles from our home in Lancaster, Pennsylvania. I hoped that a haircut would be the best short-term superficial remedy for his recent fatigue; the silver strands were growing more quickly than the brown ones lately, making him look much older than his forty-four years. The salt-and-pepper tufts brushing his starched white oxford cloth shirt robbed the usual attention from his trademark shining eyes and near-perfect smile. I also hoped that we would be able to get away to visit my parents in Marco Island, Florida, again when the children were on vacation at the end of the month. That night, the outline of his small oval face was lost in the darkened garage. Only the reflection of his glasses shone through the driver's side window.

David barely slid one foot out of the heavy car door when I heard him mutter, "Oh... I forgot the haircut. I'll go now."

He sounded exhausted, so I automatically answered in a

supportive voice, "Bye, I love you!" We religiously parted with these treasured words. They were the last utterance we made to each other every night in our simple two-story colonial house in the suburbs. The Waltons would have smiled.

He answered back, "I love you—will be back soon."

Reminiscing now, I desperately wish that I had burst through the flimsy screen door and kissed him and felt his strong arms around me.

The shish kabobs had remained on the grill too long. The cherry tomatoes were dried out and the tiny yellow seeds stuck tenaciously to the greasy, blackened metal grid. The thin skins of the green peppers were shriveled and darkened like the worn hands of an elderly fisherman. My stomach churned and head throbbed in anticipation of David's return. Intuitively I could feel that something was very wrong. It was well past the time he should have returned from the barber, who was just two miles away.

As if following an unspoken directive, I closed the lid on the propane grill and turned off the gas. Standing alone on the cold brick patio, my attention was diverted to the flashing red lights below the hillside of our neighborhood. Without the summer foliage, my view was clear for several miles. Then I heard the whine of the sirens in the distance; the high-pitched, disjointed rhythm pierced deeply into my soul and sliced at my heart. Those sounds were intended only for my ears that night as I stood motionless, frozen in time.

The sorrowful cry for help from the rescue vehicles directed me to the phone to confirm my worst fear. After my initial inquiry it seemed like hours until the local police called me back.

Twenty long minutes ticked by, and then, with the news of the accident ringing in my ears, I raced frantically upstairs to our bedroom. Our children, twelve-year-old Samantha and ten-year-old Richard, were happily playing and watching TV in the basement, unaware of my panic. I threw myself onto our bed, clutching our wedding photo and tearfully begging God not to let the news be true. But in my heart I knew it *was* true. And my prayers would not be answered. My flowing tears and heaving sobs dampened the soft down comforter as I tried to escape from my reality into its warm innocence.

After wiping my swollen face with a cold washcloth to erase the traces of my smeared mascara and smudged lipstick, I retreated downstairs. Standing before the closed basement door, I gathered all of my remaining courage. From below came the cheerful voices of our children as they awaited their father's return for dinner. Fear and danger were never their companions; for them, the world had always been safe, secure, and perfect.

I took a very long and deep breath, as if I were going to dive into the deep end of a pool and touch the bottom. I had to tell them. We needed to get to the hospital to meet the ambulance. Painfully. I descended the twelve carpeted stairs—one step at a time. Once again instinct took over and

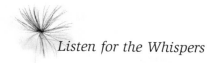

a strange calm returned to my voice. "Dad's been in an accident...we need to go to the hospital right away," I peacefully announced.

Sam and Rick had been focused on their favorite TV sit-com when I came into view. At first they did not hear me and continued lying on their stomachs with their feet waving in the air, laughing at the show. Then simultaneously, they jerked their heads around as one and said in unison, "Is he hurt?" Fear replaced the joy in their clear blue eyes and they reached for one another's tiny pink hands.

"Yes, I am afraid so," I responded with caution.

"Is he alive?" they inquired, cutting right to the severity of the moment.

"Of course—don't worry," I reassured them tentatively. Since I was not yet sure of their dad's exact injuries, I tried to protect them as best as I could.

Like robots reacting to an electronic command, the three of us marched upstairs and silently prepared to leave. The kitchen table was set for four with colorful vinyl placemats and plastic napkin rings. Over-cooked soggy French fries remained atop the stove. It was as if everything had been frozen in time by the cold February night. I gently ushered the children out the front door and into the driveway, where a car was waiting for us.

Chapter III

The Diagnosis

"Quadriplegic...." The doctor's faint whisper of the diagnosis was inevitable.

It was a cold, clear night. The stars twinkled far out in the endless darkness as if to signal the existence of life beyond. Their tiny beams pierced the opaque veil of uncertainty like hopeful glimmers. Shock and trepidation muted all sounds, so the ride to Lancaster General Hospital was in silence. Even though I had previously traveled this road so many times, it seemed so long and unfamiliar.

Sherri, my husband's secretary since our relocation to Lancaster in 1977, piloted the car with determination. Only a few years younger than me, she and her husband Craig, a dairy farmer, had a daughter and son close in age to ours. She and I often shared kid stories when I called the office, and we always marveled over how fast our children were growing when we were together at our annual Christmas parties and family summer picnics at the local pool. Now her freshly washed blonde hair hung limply on her shoulders. Because we did not have any family in the area, I had frantically called her after I spoke with the police. Sherri and David maintained a special relationship well beyond secretary and boss. Although her formal education did not equal his, she was extremely capable and a quick study. Sherri understood his complex organizational systems and disjointed thoughts, which made them a good team. Thankfully, she was loyal enough to leave her young family to be with mine.

The automatic doors welcomed us into the emergency room entrance at Lancaster General at 7:30 p.m. We reluctantly accepted the unwanted invitation. My initial call to the hospital to confirm David's arrival and condition was uninformative. Surely there was a policy that prevented hospital personnel from giving bad news over the phone, but it offended me. As we were guided into the private family waiting area, I concluded that the news would not be good. The intimate, well-decorated space off to the side of the vast, antiseptic general waiting room kept curious onlookers from invading the privacy of families in crisis. I found the artificial living room-like atmosphere of warmth and hospitality irritating as I attempted to focus my thoughts and maintain my composure. I sat quietly on the love seat with my arms around both children while Sherri waited respectfully in the general area.

My face was expressionless. Normally my blood pressure was quite low, but now I felt it drop even further, giving my heart a needed moment of rest. Perhaps I was in a state of shock and did not realize it. My body's defenses must have been sheltering me from further harm while the events played out in slow motion like clips from a scary movie.

Because of his medical history, I knew that David's injuries would be life-threatening and, most likely, a spinal injury would be involved. He had a rare arthritic condition called ankolosing spondylitis. A wise internist in Lancaster made the first diagnosis through a series of blood tests right after we were married. In the early years of the disease, he would have to sleep in an upright position propped up by large pillows in order to keep the pressure off his sciatica nerve—the first nerve to be affected by this ailment. Later on in our relationship, he would occasionally resort to sleeping in the recliner in order to ease his pain and not disturb my own rest. Slowly the discomfort traveled to other nerve endings and moved up his spine.

This time bomb was carefully filed away in the recesses of each of our minds after the diagnosis. David worked hard to lead a full and normal life, and I worked hard to forget his condition. But pain was his constant companion, an unwanted visitor that stubbornly wouldn't go away.

Surreptitiously, my husband's daily activities were reduced as his spinal column gradually calcified. "A bamboo spine" was the layman's term for this rare condition. When viewing the X-ray, it appeared like a long hollow stalk of bamboo connected with fragile bony growths. Sadly, David had to retire early from what could have been a distinguished naval career as a result of this disability. He never overtly expressed his disappointment, but I could detect the sadness in his eyes when his children admired his fancy dress-blue uniform adorned with shiny medals and colorful ribbons. A plastic model of a P-3 submarine surveillance plane he had assembled in memory of his flying days was displayed in a bookshelf at work flanked by two oak-framed pictures of him with his crew. These were pictures of my husband in his younger, healthier days dressed in his olive-green Navy flight jumpsuit, leaning against the side of his plane like a hero home from battle. A dark bushy mustache disguised his face somewhat, but the twinkle in his Irish eyes unmistakably identified him. Eventually his aviation dreams had to be vicariously lived through adventure novels and reruns of his favorite movie, *Top Gun*. How hard it must have been to give up his true passion.

David and I had enjoyed fifteen magical years of marriage highlighted by moments of clairvoyance. We had the special inner connection of soul mates. At times, I felt I knew him better than he knew himself. I would tease him that I had "special powers" and could summon them whenever he needed them. As a small-town attorney, his job was an adversarial one laced with daily conflicts and problems. He represented hope for those facing job-related injuries or financial ruin due to an accident, often at the expense of his own solace. He provided comfort and intelligent answers to complex personal situations, and he gave his clients peace of mind—serving as a surrogate set of strong shoulders when, in fact, his own were weary.

On occasion, when I observed my husband struggling internally with a particular case, I would step in to offer my unique services. I lightheartedly would tell him that I could

make everything work out all right if he wished. Sometimes he would smile dubiously, nod, and allow me to feel a sense of contribution as I assured him that everything would be fine. Afterward, when he went off to work, I would audibly ask God to watch over him and lead him swiftly to the correct answers. I wasn't asking Him to tip the blind scales of justice in my husband's favor; it was just a gentle request for a swift solution. I knew that God was always listening, and I trusted His presence. Finally, when David returned home from a challenging day, he would look at me skeptically and remark, "Curiously, everything worked out well today." He would then pause and add with a laugh, "I don't want to know what it is that you do because I am afraid that it will all go away. Just don't use it up too soon."

I felt rewarded by the trust David placed in my shared inner thoughts. My husband was dedicated to helping others, and I was dedicated to helping him.

Two doctors slowly walked into the small waiting room. I recognized them only by the plastic nameplates on their lab coats. Since David specialized in personal injury work, these two physicians knew him both professionally and personally. A respected member of the local Bar, he was not an anonymous patient lying helplessly on a stretcher that cold winter night. I could detect the genuine sadness in both of their eyes. As the osteopathic surgeon told me how David's spinal cord was severed at the base of his neck by his splintered vertebrae between C-4 and C-5, sympathetic tears appeared. He deliberately pronounced the word "quadriplegic." The syllables clung emphatically on his lips like bitter pitch seeping from a damaged pine.

I accepted the diagnosis without emotion or tears of my own. It was not a surprise to me and its proclamation was not offensive. Hours earlier I had already accepted the unspoken *whisper* and began processing its impact. Although the medical terminology was beyond their elementary comprehension, Samantha and Richard quietly sobbed and panic filled their eyes as they looked to me for hope. I calmly tried to assure them that everything would be all right, even though in my heart I knew that it would not. The earthly time with my life partner would soon be over.

This was an occasion when I would rather not have had my life script racing though my mind at an uncontrollable speed. It was difficult to be able to sense the outcome and then pretend to be unaware. There were more tests and X-rays to be completed in order to medically confirm the diagnosis. But spiritually, for me it was definite. These procedures would require hours and my assistance was not needed. I couldn't do anything more for my husband now, so with the immediate paperwork completed, I felt an urgency to return home with the children to shelter them from further distress. It was after 10 p.m. by the time Sherri drove us back to 1036 Signal Hill Lane. Silent again on the way home, the children and I clung to one another in the backseat, processing the crisis on our own levels of understanding. Sherri dropped us off in the darkened driveway, where her strong lingering embrace took the place of any comforting words. I knew she sensed impending doom and a menacing fault line threatening her friendship with her boss.

Reluctantly, I made a few necessary phone calls to alert immediate family members of the tragedy. David's parents were the first. Late-night phone calls rarely signal good news, but I needed to connect our hearts. His mother's gentle, sleepy voice stirred with fear as she pressed me for answers and hope. My next call was to David's twenty-year-old son, my stepson, a junior at Penn State's main campus in State College, who I first met as an active, towheaded four-year-old crouched skeptically in the cargo area of his dad's Pinto station wagon. He sounded so childlike and far away in the center of the state as he vowed to leave his midterms and come as quickly as possibly the next day to help me. With each call came more tears and heavy sobs on both ends of the receiver. It was so difficult not to be able to see the faces of my loved ones and to be able to hold on to one another for support. The long-distance communication only added to my isolation and fear on that late February evening. I felt so weak. There was no one there to comfort me.

I stopped after I called my own parents at their winter home in Marco Island, Florida, and then I crawled with my children into my queen-size bed. I adhered myself to Samantha and Richard all night. It was almost as if an invisible protective shell was beginning to develop. The fluffy, warm goose-down comforter that had absorbed my tears

now insulated us from danger. The fragments of our crumbled strengths bonded together to help us survive the long night as one. In the days that followed, we would sift for more bits of inner fortitude like golden nuggets in a miner's pan.

We were healing, but it was a slow and focused process. That year we did not even notice when spring arrived.

Chapter IV

Hospitals

"Tell my wife that I can't hang on any longer... I want to die now," David whispered to his nurse in the middle of the night.

Until David's accident, hospitals used to hold a certain excitement for me. I had only stayed in one twice in my life and each of my visits was a joyous occasion. Twice I waddled through the emergency entrance in the early morning hours full of excitement and anticipation as a mother-to-be. Several days later, and a few pounds lighter, I proudly exited with a warm bundle of joy, a new little person to love and cherish. This time the experience was not in any way a celebration of life—quite the contrary, in fact. I was not the patient, and I was not on the maternity floor surrounded by pink and blue blankets and Mylar balloons heralding "New Baby." Ultimately, I would not leave with one more life for which to care, one more person to love.

My husband was admitted to the Neuro Intensive Care Unit at Lancaster General Hospital, where he was connected to a series of complicated monitors via an unfriendly web of wires and clear plastic tubes. His head was anchored in place with cold, hard steel screws attached to a cumbersome metal halo. "Halo"…such a curious name given to this restrictive piece of modern hardware. The angels in heaven must cringe at this analogy to their celestial adornments.

David's car had mysteriously veered off the road and overturned on his way home from the barber. It was a one-car accident and he was the only victim. Since there were no witnesses, a cause was never determined. Using my newfound ability to communicate with David by reading his lips, he conveyed to me that he only recalled a set of bright headlights coming toward him. An examination of the car did not show any mechanical malfunction, and the roadway—although narrow and curvy, with a steep berm—was dry and clear that night. The cause of the accident will forever be a mystery to me. Sometimes I wonder if this was meant to be.

When I first saw David lying prone on the pristine white sheets of his hospital bed, he was motionless. He looked so peaceful at first. Aside from the complicated metal enclosure around his head, there was no outward sign of his tragic accident. There were no visible cuts or bruises to alert me to his injuries and summon my distress. I reached down instinctively to hold his hand as I had done so many times since our marriage. His shiny gold wedding band felt cold in my warm, trembling hand, and he didn't return my grasp.

The reality was irrefutable: my husband couldn't override the loss of connection between his body and brain.

David's steel-blue eyes darted back and forth across the

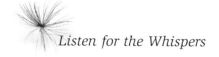

curtained space. I knew that his mind was racing at the speed of light. Fortunately, he remained conscious and in complete mental control; his high level of intelligence and clever reasoning skills were his gifts and the tools of his profession. Now he was trapped in his own damaged body, alone with his thoughts and overcome by guilt. I doubt that any prison sentence could be more severe and harsh in its punishment. He mouthed the words "I'm sorry! I love you!" slowly and deliberately. There was no audible sound but I understood the message.

Just as in his law practice, we were facing a deadline—tragically, the final one for the two of us. There would be no opportunity for drawn-out intellectual discussions or speculation as to the cause of the accident. There was no time for long explanations or in-depth analyses, no time to reminisce.

Unconditional love was all that I could offer David to ease the emotional pain. His physical pain had ceased with the splitting of his spinal cord. My natural curiosity and inquisitive nature had to be restrained; I needed to put aside my own selfish desires and give over my absolute attention. My season would come later, when I was alone. Right now the ticking minutes were my enemy—and they catapulted me into action.

I stroked his unshaven face and gently assured him that no apologies for anything were needed. "I love you too," I responded loudly.

We needed to share our love in our own ways. His parched lips parted to allow his tongue to reach out desperately and stroke the back of my hand. This was his only way to "hold" me; it was a vibrant and warm sensation as it twisted between my fingers like a minnow in a rocky stream. Our eyes locked frequently. Words were never exchanged again; we didn't need them anymore. We now communicated on a higher level as our souls merged.

As the hours passed, I could feel the ebb and flow of my strength like the strong undertow of the North Carolina coastline where we vacationed with his parents and brother's family one summer. Back and forth it went, dragging me along, eventually leaving me to drift aimlessly. There were so many urgent decisions to make. My husband's life was actually resting in my hands.

"Help me!" David desperately continued to form the words with his muted mouth. This plea was both uncharacteristic and unnerving. David had always been such a proud and independent man. He had never asked me for help before in our fifteen-year marriage. I was not a doctor and certainly didn't know anything about spinal cord injuries. Yet I did know that my husband, my life partner, was anxiously reaching out to me. Although he was no longer physically intact, he was still a formidable individual who deserved dignity and respect. I couldn't possibly run away, but I was scared and frantically wanted to hide and protect myself from the demands I was facing. For a moment I pretended that it was a bad dream. Silently I prayed that I would wake up and be back in my familiar cozy kitchen making dinner. I closed my eyelids tightly, attempting to

block out all outwards signs of trouble. Yet the fibers of my soul were tethered to David's and the reality of our situation.

My sister Jill, number three in a pecking order of four girls in a middle-class family from upstate New York, was a registered oncology nurse in New York City. Upon learning of my husband's accident she immediately drove from her home in Scarsdale, New York, to assist me with David's medical decisions. Family became my external strength. I always knew that I had a very special family but it was never put to such a test. Jill arrived with an incredible network of contacts compiled with the aid of her able husband Richard—ranging from the names of physicians at Stanford University Hospital to phone numbers of doctors at New York's prestigious Mount Sinai Hospital. Her expertise and continuous love and support resuscitated my weakened spirit.

It was Jill who orchestrated David's move to Philadelphia's Thomas Jefferson University Hospital, a regional spinal cord treatment center for the East Coast. She gave me the courage and confidence to confront his local doctors and to insist upon his transfer to the specialized facility. I still cringe at my final display of controlled defiance in the face of the four attending physicians on the morning of our anticipated departure from Lancaster General. The doctors continued to be in disagreement with my insistence to move my husband and wanted to continue applying other life-saving techniques. Beneath their white lab coats and pale green scrubs were talented, intelligent men trying to offer the best medical care they could, but I was being driven again by my non-professional instincts and abundant love for my husband.

As I stood within this semi-circle of towering authority in the intensive care unit, I announced, "He is my husband and I am moving him now!" They respectfully heard me out and perhaps quietly dismissed my demand as the incoherent words of a desperate and irrational woman. Time was peeking over my shoulder and I needed to transfer David as quickly as possible. Hours meant hope, and I wasn't going to waste even a minute. Bureaucratically, I needed the consent and agreement of all his physicians for this change of venue since, at this point in his two-day care, I couldn't just wheel his limp body out of the hospital on my own. Like a child waiting for a turn to speak, I needed their permission to continue on our final journey. Within moments my persistence paid off and they all reluctantly agreed to my request.

As the technicians and nurses prepared for David's transfer by helicopter, I assured him that he would be receiving the best possible care at Jefferson. He looked nervous but relieved that I heard his *whisper* for help. We both knew that a miracle was not going to happen; this was about buying more time together to complete our circle of life. A small crowd of family members, medical personnel, and supporters gathered around his gurney to wish him well on the short flight. Sadly, Samantha, Richard, and young David would only see their father alive one more time.

Plastic tubes were set in place around my husband, with

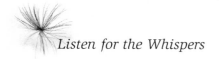

foam blocks securing his head like the packaging of a muse-um artifact; in reality it was equally as precious, since it was the only part of his body that continued to function on its own. Pouches of A negative blood donated by me and David's family members was stored chilled in insulated boxes, ready to be pumped into his veins when needed. (Curiously, liquids can be transferred from one body to anoth-er in order to sustain life, but as of yet we have not discov-ered how to return life to otherwise healthy dormant limbs.)

"Don't forget the medicine!" I panicked. Jill networked across the country and obtained a valuable supply of the experimental drug Sygen. It was the same miracle nerve-regenerating substance administered to New York Jet's foot-ball player Dennis Byrd, who faced paralysis after breaking his C-5 vertebra during a 1992 match. The drug had to be administered within seventy-two hours after the injury and we were fast approaching the final hours of that window. We needed to move quickly.

During the confusion in the ICU, I noticed a tall, bald, imposing figure by the exit in a dark green zippered flight suit and mirrored aviator glasses. My familiarity with David's role as a tactical navigator in the Naval Reserves helped me recognize that he was probably the pilot of the waiting helicopter. He represented my escape to hope. I walked over to him to introduce myself. He kindly expressed his condolences about the accident and assured me that the flight would be a smooth one. I wanted to trav-el along with David in the Lifeline Helicopter, but aside from my husband, the cramped quarters of the cabin could only accommodate the pilot, an attending physician from Jefferson, and his medical assistant. At 2:25 p.m., as I left the hospital parking lot in my maroon Toyota Camry, the sound of the whirling blades hovered simultaneously above me. In a way, David and I were leaving together.

This thought gave me momentary comfort as I watched the mechanical bird climb high in the sky over Lancaster. Was he climbing higher to be closer to God, I worried, or would we have a few more days together on earth?

By the time my step-son and I arrived at Thomas Jefferson Hospital four hours later, after getting lost in Philadelphia looking for the hospital at Tenth and Walnut streets, David was hooked up to a series of weights and pulleys. Dr. Jerome Cotler, the head of the Regional Spinal Cord Center, had invented a device called a vector traction, which externally manipulates the disrupted bones of the vertebrae back into alignment. This odd contraption dominated a fluorescent-lit room like a giant tinker toy, with a human body trapped and suspended in the middle. Its juxtaposition of metal cables, weights, and pulleys was beyond my comprehension, and it seemed to me as if the device should have been sitting in an auto mechanic's garage mending the tangled pieces of a damaged car—not attached to my husband's body like a bad science fiction movie.

In my husband's case, this extreme equipment precluded the need for an invasive procedure that would open him

up to a potentially dangerous infection. When we entered David's room, his twisted spine already was so close to proper alignment that further assessment could be made to determine the actual spinal cord damage.

David looked very nervous. I tried to read his thoughts, but my wide-eyed stare unnerved him even more. He tried to comfort me by mouthing the words, "Don't worry, it's okay." He was so brave, so courageous.

The head surgeon at Thomas Jefferson Hospital told me that he had only seen a handful of cases similar to ours in his long career. This gentle, grandfatherly man was generous with his valuable time and I appreciated his quiet and calm manner. I felt that he was truly receptive to my questions and responded honestly. Although I had just met him, I trusted him.

He sat down with me in his cluttered office and patiently indulged my numerous inquiries and concerns as we discussed David's condition. It was complicated. There just weren't enough studies of similar cases and medical journal articles to provide statistics and realistic projections. Why is it that we always want to know the "odds?" Why do we reduce our survival to numerical formulas? Do we really feel better if the "odds" are in our favor or should we immediately give up if they are not? Because David's case was so novel, it was featured in the next day's hospital staff meeting. I even signed a release to permit drawings of David's neck and spinal column by a medical artist for future journals. Since we didn't know how to help ourselves, perhaps we could help someone else in the future.

My husband and I felt extremely alone now in this new territory, with no coordinates to guide us. Love and mutual trust were our only signals; a *whisper* was the sextant. David's job in the Navy had been to chart the course and guide his crew safely on their journey. I now had to assume this role in our life together. I was the navigator.

Thirteen days had passed since the accident. David's condition progressively worsened while more machines and yards of tubes filled his private room. His diminished lungs, weakened from years of reduced capacity due to his illness, were barely staying oxygenated by the humming ventilator. His heart, however, remained strong and continued to beat under its own power. His mind was remarkably clear, filled with extraordinary determination. But ultimately his spirit was growing weary. The dedicated and wonderful ICU nurses at Jefferson brought ice chips to soothe his dry mouth. Nutrients were absorbed through thin blue tubes bypassing his mouth and going straight into his stomach. Pain medication eased the resurgence of spasms from the few raw nerve endings at the base of his skull. Meanwhile, his anguish and guilt kept resurfacing.

Recently, my husband had been involved in the emerging area of living wills and advance directives. He organized a committee at our church to inform parishioners of the legalities of this issue while the pastors wrestled with the spiritual side. Predictably, he took care of everyone else's

business first and did not have a living will of his own. I did not even have a durable power of attorney for critical medical decisions.

In his heart, David knew the end was near. And I had known it for days. But who would speak first? Since my husband had initially asked me for help at the beginning of this ordeal, I felt that I had to be the leader.

I leaned over the rotor bed that methodically cradled his fluid-filled body from side to side in an artificial attempt to promote circulation and prevent blood clots. "Are you ready to die?" I casually asked him, taking control of the situation. The words slipped out effortlessly as if I were asking him what he wanted for dinner.

The look on his face was one of relief and gratitude. "Yes," he mouthed gingerly, "I want to die," he affirmed.

"That's fine," I responded casually. "I will help you to die with dignity."

David's eyes crinkled up on the sides and his whole face smiled. "I knew you would," he mouthed.

My husband had always joked that my German-Scotch heritage gave me the nature of a rat terrier. When given a task, I wouldn't give up until I shook the life out of it. And I wouldn't give up now until his last breath left with the dignity it deserved. But how? Again, I was in uncharted waters…alone.

Chapter V

The Ethics Committee

"It's all right.... You can go now...,"
I whispered.

A "do not resuscitate" order for David had been granted at our request on the fourteenth day after the accident, his final day at Thomas Jefferson University Hospital. To both of us it seemed so logical, since we knew that his life was quickly coming to an end. Our earthly union soon would be severed like the delicate fibers of his spinal cord, yet I quietly assured him that I would be fine. I could feel his strength transferring to me as he smiled in agreement.

The insignificant metal ventilator dutifully hummed away, forcing fresh oxygen into his tired lifeless body. Liquid nourishment was transferred by clear plastic tubes while cloudy waste was carried out by another network of hoses. The quality of his life was gone; my husband was merely renting space now. For twelve days he had been lying on a sterile, foreign bed away from his loving family and familiar home. His accident and medical condition had taken over his identity as reams of papers filled with medical statistics became the doctors' focus. Gone was the familiar aroma of his pungent pine cologne. Gone was the fragrant mixture of spicy shaving cream and freshly starched shirts wafting past my face in the early mornings. Everything was so antiseptic and impersonal. The prevailing odor of plastic and disinfectant dulled my olfactory senses and will forever linger in my memory.

Without the proper paperwork, hospital regulations prevent the discontinuance of life support. I understood the necessary safeguards firsthand, since conversely I had fought desperately for all of the available life-saving technology just a few days earlier. Now, I was frustrated by their presence. They were all the barriers of my promise to my husband.

"Joe, I need your help. David wants to die."

On the pivotal date of February 24, 1993, I had placed the call to my husband's legal mentor from the privacy of the pay phone booth in the hallway of the Neuro Intensive Care Unit. Joe was "Foster," the sage lawyer for whom David had worked at the law firm of White and Williams, our first meeting place. Sixteen years had passed since we left the office together to start a new life, and while I had not seen Joe since, David's practice intersected with his on occasion. Joe was a powerful and well-respected defense attorney in the Philadelphia Bar Association. I gambled that he would be willing to help us, since he and David had developed a mutual respect for each other during their long days at 1234 Market Street. They both ran their fingers through their graying, thin hair and puffed away on cigarettes while preparing late into the night for upcoming trials.

Although almost two decades separated them chronologically, they were a like a mismatched set of twins.

Plunging forward, I gave Joe a brief summary of the accident and its aftermath over the phone. He respected brevity, so I stuck to the facts. There was momentary silence on the other end, then his familiar gruff voice: "My God! I'll help you with whatever you need." He subsequently confided that several years ago, he, too, had had a frightening brush with death at this very same place. After his successful cancer surgery, he gave the institution a hefty donation in gratitude for his extraordinary treatment—and now he was prepared to cash in his generosity for his friend David. I would have to meet with the prestigious Hospital Ethics Committee, he told me, and it was going to be difficult to do on such short notice. He would make some phone calls on my behalf.

While perched on the seat in the cramped phone booth, I began to reflect upon the last few days' events. So much effort was being dedicated to artificially prolonging a cycle that was near its logical conclusion. All David wanted was the opportunity to die naturally, with dignity.

The loud ringing of the phone startled me back to the present. Joe was calling after an eternity that had only been twenty minutes. He had succeeded in arranging a meeting of the Ethics Committee for 2:00 that very afternoon. I never doubted his dedication to our cause, but I was surprised by its speed and outcome. The Ethics Committee was an elite group of esteemed physicians and hospital department heads at Jefferson who held sway over all critical patient decisions. They ultimately decided who would be required to continue living medically and who would be permitted to slip away naturally. When I brought the news of the meeting to David's bedside, his tired eyes lacked their familiar glow. But I could tell he was pleased. "Good luck," he slowly mouthed. For a moment I could feel myself wrestling with my commitment to proceed, but I had promised to help, not to question.

Vanessa, my youngest sister by three years, had an uncanny way of appearing during this ordeal at the most important moments. Her demanding life as a Wall Street financial analyst never prevented her from being at my side when I needed her, and I appreciated the support. Vanessa had traveled several times by train from Manhattan to keep me company in the hospital in Philadelphia. Sometimes we sat in supportive silence for hours in the lonely waiting room, hoping for good news. Other times we stood next to David's bed, watching him rest while awaiting an opportunity to say hello. When we were hungry, we ate at the hospital cafeteria on the ground floor. And then she would depart on the train once again to be with her family.

The stage was now set. Vanessa, Joe, and I met at the hospital's main elevator at 1:45 p.m., just before the meeting, and rode together to the top floor. Joe wasn't there for legal support but came as a friend. Vanessa was there as my loyal sister. The elevator trip was made in silence, with each of us consumed by private thoughts.

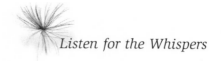

As the heavy steel doors opened, sunshine streamed in. Directly in front of me was a well-marked exit to the roof-top helicopter pad. Twelve days earlier, I noted sadly, David had arrived at this very location from Lancaster. Joe led us down the narrow carpeted hallway to a set of carved wooden doors. "Wait here," he instructed, "they will call us in when they are ready." Shortly, a serious-looking man in an expensive dark suit opened the doors and ushered us in. Twenty-four men sat rigidly and evenly spaced around an oval table of polished mahogany. Sunlight reflected off of its shiny surface, creating a mirror-like image. As a result, there were forty-eight strange faces staring at us without a trace of emotion. The windows afforded a slightly disjointed panorama of Philadelphia, reminding me of an immense urban jigsaw puzzle. Three plush upholstered seats remained vacant at the near end of the table. I sat down first, then Vanessa and finally Joe. The human circle closed tightly.

Prior to our arrival, the committee head had given the necessary medical background. Now the formal hearing would begin. David's attending physician was seated at the very far end of the table. This middle-aged group member was the only one in the room who had actually met my husband. He consulted with me periodically during our stay, and just hours before, he and I met in David's room to confirm our decision. The doctor was about the same age as David and probably had a wife and a young family just like his patient, and he temporarily stepped away from his medical role to listen to our message as human beings. I sensed that he respected my husband's difficult decision as he took the time to look into David's eyes. My husband's eyes were so expressive; his conviction was unmistakable as he blinked back in agreement to the doctor's words.

Sitting before the committee, I found an unlikely part of my background coming into play. My first declared major at Washington College was theatre. I always loved to entertain others and still foolishly do. As a skinny young girl, I often danced in our private backyard in funny, old dress-up clothes, pretending that the surrounding shrubs were hundreds of spectators—and I bowed to their silent approval upon my finale. I had several small roles during my freshman year at college and continued to look for little opportunities to step into the intoxicating limelight. Now, David had given me the ultimate opportunity for my consummate performance. Six stories below he lay motionless and unable to watch the show. But I knew that a part of him was really with me, front row. He had entrusted me with his fate. There was no dress rehearsal for this performance, no second chance.

At first the words hesitantly slipped from my mouth. I could feel my throat tighten in an effort to vocalize my carefully prepared thoughts. My first intention was to introduce my husband, the person, to these skeptical strangers. I wanted them to know the man, not just the patient with the unique medical condition in NICU Room #2.

Their expressionless eyes stared directly at me, focusing

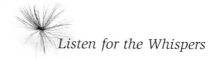

on my face like laser beams locked on a target. They questioned our relationship and the quality of his physical being during our marriage. They explored the concept of the possibility of a future life as a quadriplegic.

To me the inquiries were irrelevant. Dignity and respect were the primary issues for us. Couldn't these fellow human beings see that that this was not a decision that was made easily? It was not one made in reaction to the two weeks' continuous pain and suffering, as one physician suggested. The time had simply run out. His spirit was not mine to lock up and hold hostage like a priceless treasure. Nor was his body theirs to artificially sustain in a small antiseptic room far from home.

Forty long minutes later, I finished my monologue and the curtain came down. The entire committee dutifully thanked me and assured me that they would make their decision in a timely fashion.

As it would turn out, the decision was never theirs to make.

Joe, Vanessa, and I rode one last time together down in the modest elevator. Just as during our ascent, each of us was preoccupied with our own thoughts. When we returned to the Intensive Care Unit, David's sweet young nurse rushed to tell me that my husband's heart had already stopped once about five minutes earlier. Because of the "do not resuscitate" order no action was taken, but under David's own power it had restarted—and he was now in a state of semi-consciousness. I quickly calculated the time in my head. My speech had ended precisely five minutes ago. He had come back for us to say goodbye one last time!

Joe, who had informally introduced David and I to each other in 1976, was there now to watch as our union withered—casting a long shadow across my heart. Vanessa had been present on New Year's Eve of that same year, when David proposed to me in the kitchen of my small apartment in Newtown Square. She, too, would now be witness to fate's dissolution of our marriage.

David was staring straight ahead with a glazed look. He did not physically respond to my voice with the usual blink or smile. I remembered that my sister Jill once told me that the very last of the five senses to leave a dying person's body was the sense of hearing. She worked extensively with geriatric cancer patients and stressed the importance of communication, even when it seemed futile.

I leaned over my husband's still body and *whispered*, "It's all right now, David, they listened. It was a good show. You can go now. I love you."

Minutes later, the line went flat on the EKG monitor. David didn't have to wait for a formal proclamation from the Hospital Ethics Committee. Instead, he took charge one last time and parted with his dignity intact.

Chapter VI

Till Death Do Us Part

"It was beautiful... Such bright lights," was the whisper of hope.

The hospital room was uncomfortably silent. I looked nervously at my sister Vanessa. Joe knelt at David's side to say a prayer as his final goodbye. With a drawn and sorrowful face, he expressed his condolences and showed his respect for our privacy with his departure.

The respirator had stopped humming artificial breath and the EKG monitor no longer beeped and signaled each heartbeat. At 4:20 p.m., my husband, David Stewart Kluxen Jr., had died.

I had never been alone with a dead person before, but I wasn't scared because it wasn't a stranger lying there. I intimately knew my husband in life, and now I was introduced to him in death. The hollow wooden door to his private room was closed tightly, and it was just the three of us: Vanessa, David, and me. Quietly I asked my sister what we should do next. Both of us were well into our adult lives without much funeral experience and were quite shaken. Should we run out in a panic and announce his demise? Should I pull out all of the unnecessary tubes and wires so that it would look like he was only sleeping? Out of complete exhaustion and nervousness, we both burst out in quiet laughter. It was not an irreverent comical moment meant to diminish the sacredness of the event, but instead it was an uncontrolled release for our fragile and stressed emotions, which had been rigorously tested for the past two weeks. It was as if a tremendous weight had been lifted off my shoulders; suppressed emotions and stifled tears erupted. We must have looked very strange in that moment.

The late-afternoon sunlight bathed David's face in serene amber, creating an aura of peacefulness I did not want to disturb. His struggle was over and the pain was gone forever. My sister and I continued to stare at the monitors as if awaiting a signal for our next move; none came. I leaned over my husband for the last time, caressing his smooth, tranquil face and placing a gentle kiss on his lukewarm lips. We were truly separated, for now.

The day before David's death, I had reluctantly met with the hospital social worker. This required meeting was arranged in order to help me to cope with my family's ordeal. First, we casually discussed his updated condition, and then I cautiously shared with this woman my unusual intuition. I told her confidently that David was going to die the next day. She looked at me skeptically and asked how I could know such a thing. "I just know," I said. Intellectually it probably wasn't possible, but for me it was very real.

On my commute that morning from Lancaster to Philadelphia, my attention was directed to the clear morning

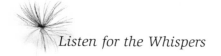

sky. The clouds were white and puffy like mounds of sugary meringue. Slowly out of one of the largest clouds appeared the silvery outline of a jet plane. Climbing higher and higher, the trace of its plume left a faint white path to the heavens. David loved to fly, I thought, smiling to myself. Symbolically for me, that vision represented my husband's imminent journey toward Heaven. Higher and higher the plane went until it disappeared into the atmosphere beyond my world. The sight comforted me and reminded me that we had peacefully come to terms with David's eventual death. Perhaps it was my simple way of rationalizing the complications of the situation. I did not tell the social worker what I saw and how I had interpreted it. I did not want her to think that I was crazy and write down more notes on her clipboard for our expanding file. I just told her simply that I felt that my husband was going to die the next day. She may have thought I had given up. But I had never given up. I just knew the end was here.

February 24, 1993, was Ash Wednesday. It was the beginning of the Lenten season that marked the seven Wednesdays before Easter in the Christian faith. How befitting this was! This special spiritual holiday is a day that reminds Christians all over the world of the power of God's forgiveness. It reminds us that as humans, we sometimes hurt one another and disappoint God. As we confess these sins and admit our shortcomings, we receive His forgiveness and understanding. Every day that I saw David after the accident, the first words to appear on his lips were, "I'm sorry." But never for a moment did I assign any fault to him. It was an accident. He had my forgiveness from the moment I saw him in the emergency room in Lancaster. Now, on this very special religious day, I was sure that he had God's forgiveness, too.

Death is the final chapter of life that each one of us must face alone. Our beginning is a protected, guided journey through the womb as we leave the safety of our mothers. Tethered for nine months by a lifeline of blood and nutrients, the moment the cord is cut, we are released to begin the journey called life. Just as we experience a beginning, each one of us is destined to arrive at the end someday.

My husband and I shared secretly an enlightened experience the night before his death. David was anxious to clearly mouth the words describing something so few are privy to experience while on earth. It was a true gift from him to me—our spiritual connection allowing me to understand the unspoken words of his unsettling story. Earlier, he had a terrible dream. He was unable to close his eyes in peace after an exhausting day because every time he tried, horrible, grotesque, demon-like figures would leap at his bedside trying to harm his body. He panicked at their appearance, he confided, but couldn't cry out for help or push them away. Trapped in a voiceless, motionless body, all he could do was nervously observe and pray to God for help.

The weakening muscles of David's face twitched and twisted as he rallied his remaining strength to continue this story. After what seemed like hours, he recounted, a protective

glow slowly surrounded his bed—rising from the floor to the ceiling and pushing the ominous figures back forcefully with its powerful radiance until they disappeared completely. This strong light became brighter and more intense, and then the vast illumination narrowed into a tunnel shape— drawing him closer and closer toward its source. "It was beautiful," he expressed. "Such bright lights. Such beautiful colors. It was so peaceful. I wasn't afraid anymore."

I felt a sense of relief that he had been spiritually comforted that night, but I couldn't comprehend it. Were the drugs distorting his lucidity or did he really have a glimpse of the afterlife? I chose the latter and then kept this story to myself for many months. I later concluded that the frailty of our human spirit is tested right up to the very end. David's spiritual strength and genuine kindness overrode his human faults and indiscretions and brought him to the doorstep of Heaven for a glimpse of his reward. That special shared moment will forever be with me. The incredible offering of his insight into the power and goodness of God, and the extended promise of everlasting life, has strengthened my faith and given me a sense of inner peace that to this day soothes my anxious moments and calms my worst fears. God is truly good. I believe that He does have a plan for all of us, but we just need to listen to it. Death may be the final chapter of life, but the story doesn't end there. None of us can really predict the future because we are not on that spiritual level in our human form. Although I have been given glimpses and *whispers*, there still will be surprises and disappointments. I have learned to look to the future with anticipation and hope, and I try to embrace all that it has to offer me.

The easy part was saying goodbye; the difficult part, I knew, would be to go on without him.

True survivors don't complain. I think that how we reconcile with death early on in our own lives sets the tone for our future acceptance of our own mortality. We can either be comfortable with it and accept it as a peaceful beginning to the next stage, or view it as unfair and fight it all the way. There was no doubt that, in the wake of David's passing, a piece of the fabric of my identity was gone—ripped from deep within my heart and soul. I had two options: to mend the hole with fond memories and warm feelings, with the acceptance that I was never meant to own him forever; or I could leave the tear open and vulnerable to loneliness and pain. I would choose to make it a comforting, nostalgic spot perpetuating my inner peace.

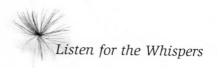

Section Two:

The Aftermath

Chapter VII

Telling the Children

"Dad died this afternoon... He will be our guardian angel from now on," *I whispered to the children.*

Feeling an odd sense of duty, Vanessa and I exited from David's room to alert the on-duty nurses of his death. Just then, my husband's forty-year-old brother Bob and his wife Barb were arriving at the hospital from their home just outside of the city for their regular visit. The first of David's immediate family to hear the sad news, they stepped into the room to say a final goodbye while Vanessa and I continued to the nurses' station.

Exhausted and emotionally drained, I explained to the hospital staff my urgent desire to go home to be with my children. Before I left, they provided me with the necessary forms to be signed and agreed to my plan. Very soon I would select a funeral home in Lancaster that would make the remaining arrangements to transfer my husband's body. Thankfully, Bob and Barb offered to drive me home. I said goodbye to Vanessa in the waiting room and she took the train back to New York City alone—only to return to Lancaster a few days later with her husband Burt for the memorial service.

On the way back from Jefferson we stopped off at Bob's house to call David's parents. I was relieved that Bob offered to make the call for me, since I didn't feel like I could carry on a conversation—let alone tell my wonderful in-laws that their eldest son had died. While Bob spoke on the phone, Barb brought me a hot cup of tea and lemon and allowed me to collect my thoughts. I was scared and overwhelmed by what I had to do next.

A short time later, alone in the back seat of their car, I stared out at the full moon in the clear black winter night. Pressing my face against the window, it seemed to follow me on my journey, lighting the way like a huge searchlight. I wondered if David could look down at me and see me staring hopefully at the sky, searching for a sign that he had arrived safely in Heaven. Could he see me huddled against the door? I *whispered* to him in my mind and asked him to help me tell the children. I couldn't imagine how I was going to inform them that their father had died. Mine was still alive. My grandfather was still alive. The order was so very wrong.

As the miles slid by, a calm feeling washed over me like a spring shower and, in a way, I felt David's support. I did not speak a word during the ninety-minute trip home, suppressing my tears with a rapid blinking motion. I didn't want to arrive with red, swollen eyes and upset Samantha and Richard more than necessary.

When we arrived at my house in Lancaster, Bob and

Barb decided not to come in with me. Again, they kindly respected my privacy and clearly understood that I had a very difficult task. Each of them having dealt with similar situations in their own families years before, they were sympathetic and truly empathetic.

I was sure the children were not anticipating this final news. On February 17th, I had taken them to Philadelphia for what would be their last visit with their father. Children were not usually allowed in the Intensive Care Unit, but I convinced the nurse that they needed to see their father. Strangely, they were not intimidated by David's unfamiliar physical condition. He was starting to retain fluids and his puffy skin was jaundiced, but he was still Dad to them. They both marched straight to his side and lovingly peered through the metal sidebars to catch a glimpse of his face. Their innocent smiles and simple words of encouragement were almost more than I could bear. They were curious about all of the machines and computers to which David was connected. At the conclusion of their short visit, they begged to take along some latex surgical gloves as souvenirs. Over the next two years, my daughter would sleep with her pair tucked under her pillow every night.

It was 9:30 p.m. when I entered the house. Samantha and Richard were happily perched on the family room couch watching the Grammy Awards with their Aunt Christine. Christine, my oldest sister, had selflessly left her husband and three daughters behind in Eureka, California, to come to my aid. By the eighth day of our crisis, she had stepped in to maintain the daily activities of our household. She and I are only eighteen months apart and our styles are very similar. Chris gave me the freedom to travel back and forth to Philadelphia as well as the peace of mind to make whatever decisions were needed. When I stayed overnight in Center City, I could rest at ease knowing that she was in Lancaster with my family.

We snuggled together as I sat down on the couch. Oddly I didn't feel like I was alone in delivering the news—I felt David with me. "I have to tell you...something sad," I started. "Dad died this afternoon. He was trying very hard to get better, but he was just too sick and was getting very weak. He is in Heaven now and will be our guardian angel."

I finished these words in a *whisper*. No medical details were necessary to clutter the devastating message. I could not imagine what their small minds were thinking or how they were processing the news about their beloved father.

Their initial reaction pleased me. "Did he say anything for us when he died?" they wondered. Family was the most important thing to David, so it was only logical that our last conversation concerned the children. "Yes," I replied quietly. I explained to them that even though their father could not speak, he and I could communicate perfectly.

I told Samantha that her father said, "Tell Sammy that I want her to be a doctor, if she wants." Even though Samantha was only in elementary school, her dad appreciated her budding intellect and the two of them had prolonged bedtime chats each evening. In the darkness, he shared his

silly jokes and even his adult frustrations. Today she is so much like him; it is evident that she has inherited David's sharp wit and clever humor.

Four years later, after Samantha finished her second year of high school, she would share with me her concerns about career choices. She said she really wanted to pursue law but told me that she couldn't. I was puzzled by the roadblock and asked her, "Why not?" She answered, "Because I told Dad that I wouldn't become a lawyer—he didn't want me to." David often expressed his frustrations with his career to me, and I tried to explain to her that he only wanted to protect his precious young daughter with his advice. I assured her that if her father could see her today that he would support her choice no matter what it was. I knew he would be extremely proud to have her follow in his footsteps. His name remains on the simple wooded sign of his partner's practice in Lancaster, Kluxen and Newcomer, like a silent invitation for Sam to join the field someday.

Rick was impatient to hear what his father's special message to him had been. "What about me?" he said. I told him what David had conveyed to me with a big smile: "Tell Rick to be a clown."

At ten years old, our youngest was a happy-go-lucky boy with a grin that was too large for his face. I could identify with his zest for life; his impish laugh was infectious. Rick brought laughter and joy to David right up to the end, and he had always inspired his father to leave behind the serious world of law and enter with him into a more innocent and carefree terrestrial sphere. When our son heard his dad's message he predictably started to laugh, just like his father. We liked to call this hearty, throaty sound the "hedgehog laugh." In that moment, it reminded us all of happier times around the kitchen table after dinner.

After about fifteen minutes of simple questions and answers, the children went casually back to watching TV. This is not to say that they were not deeply touched and were not in the initial stages of grief, but it was all that their young minds could process for now. Our healing would progress in tiny steps throughout the upcoming years, just like a young child learning to walk. Small steps make for sure footing, and our restoration continues. As the milestones in their lives erupted in our path of recovery, so did moments of sadness and reflection. First there were church confirmations, then high school entrances and proms, followed by graduations and college choices and career paths. These were events that were meant to be shared by both parents, but were now left up to me alone. They were bittersweet times for all of us.

David's oldest son, David, had been back and forth between State College and Lancaster after the accident while he tried to work through his midterm exams. His last visit with his father was on February 20, when the two of them had a long, private conversation as best they could. It was an opportunity for them to come full circle in their relationship, a very healing time. Father and son had been separated by divorce when David was four—and later by a

continent when young David moved to Oregon with his mother and new stepfather in the summer of 1978. We looked forward to our six-week annual summer visits and filled them with beach trips, miniature golf outings, and family picnics with his paternal relatives in the Philadelphia area. When I had to tell young David the final news over the phone late that night, I could feel his searing pain as he shouted out his disbelief. The two of them had just learned to appreciate each other as adults when he entered college, and now once again they were cruelly separated.

I will never truly know how the children felt about their father's death; perhaps these feelings are not mine to know. Each was at a different stage of development. I tried so hard to protect them from the hurt. Alone at night after a nostalgic Father's Day remembrance or a high school graduation party, I would cry quietly. I wanted so much to fix everything and to make it all better. But I felt so helpless, and the children's pain added another layer to my own. Previously, as a young mother, I could always make everything better. Small cuts and scrapes were quickly bandaged and minor disappointments disappeared with a special treat. I had been in control of my children's lives and could make sure that their world was happy and carefree. But with events occurring that were beyond my maternal powers, I couldn't make their sadness disappear with a Popsicle. I could never bring their father back.

One year later, when she was in the seventh grade, Samantha was assigned to write a creative essay. I was surprised that she based it upon the painful personal experience of her father's death, complete with pseudonyms and adjusted details. I was amazed at the extremely accurate observations and insight in her recollections. Here, I include her story within my story as a tribute to a very special daughter—and as a reassurance to me that I had a bit more success in making things better than I realized:

A Valuable Lesson
By Samantha Marie Kluxen

In a town far away there lived a boy named Greg. He was an average boy in the fifth grade. Like other boys in his class, he had not gotten his growth spurt and he was short. He had brown hair and blue-gray eyes. Greg was a friendly boy and his sense of humor made him quite popular. He usually played football with his friends during recess. Actually, he was quite good compared to the other boys. Greg planned to go out for the football team later that year. He lived with his mother, father, sister Amanda, and his other sister Brooke.

Greg and his family lived in comfortable house in a middle-class neighborhood. It was the kind of neighborhood where you didn't know everyone, but you were friendly with lots of people. Greg's father was a lawyer and his mother was a banker. It was a very close family. At dinner they would all eat together and listen to each other's stories about their daily events. Greg and his sisters got along well, except for occasional fights that every brother and sister have.

One day late in December, Greg, was in the basement

68

playing a game with his sister Amanda when his mother came down with Brooke. Greg could tell by his mother's pale face that something was wrong. As she sat down, she said, "Your father has been in a car accident." Then her eyes welled up with tears. After she calmed down they went upstairs. Greg's mom encouraged the kids to eat but they were all too nervous. So the dinner just remained untouched on the table. After a half hour the group bundled up and drove into the city to the hospital. It was a cold night and the wind whipped against their faces as they approached the revolving doors. Greg had never like hospitals. He had always thought that there was an eerie silence about them. Greg and his sisters waited patiently while their mother asked a nearby nurse about their father's condition. Greg's mother came back with a young nurse who led them to the Family Council Room. By then, Greg's mom's face was dead white and her blood pressure dropped very low. About a minute later a doctor came running into the room to explain their father's situation. From the look on the doctor's face, Greg could tell that he did not have good news. The doctor cleared his throat and proceeded to tell Greg and his family that their father's condition was not very good. He had broken his neck, was paralyzed from the neck down, and had a collapsed lung. He could not talk or communicate because of the tube stuck in his windpipe that provided oxygen for him to breathe. He could not breathe on his own. By now Greg's mom had not started to cry. Instead she stared straight ahead at absolutely nothing. She was in shock. The family wondered why this was happening to them. They were right to think this. Their father was a very kind person.

He went to church every Sunday and he sometimes did free legal work for people who needed it desperately but could not afford it. Greg was still in tears when they left the hospital late that night. That evening Greg, his mom, and his sisters slept in the same bed afraid and scared of what tomorrow would bring.

The next morning Greg and his family awoke around 9:00. Their untouched dinner still lay on the table. No one was hungry but their mom made them nibble on something. They were to visit their dad that day and then go to see the car that had been smashed from the accident. The family was quiet on the drive to the hospital. Their father was in the Neuro-Trauma Unit. As they walked into the hospital there was an odd familiarity. Greg was nervous and his stomach was twisting and turning, afraid of what he might find. As he approached his father's cubicle, the sound of his shoes echoed down the quiet hallway. Then, for the first time, he saw his dad. He was scared. His dad lay there silently. His head had been secured to the bed with a series of screws and a metal halo so that his neck would not move. It was horrifying to see his dad this way but he knew that he must be strong, for his family, and most importantly for his dad. Greg's sisters had reacted the same way that Greg had. Their faces were white, their knees were wobbling, and their eyes were beginning to water. Their mother acted differently. She went right over to their dad and began stroking his face and talking to him. He had feeling from his neck up. Eventually, the whole family started talking to him. He just kept mouthing the words, "I love you." The family left the hospital later that morning. They then went to see the car.

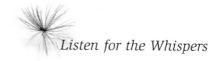

Greg's mom remarked that it was almost harder to look at the car than it was to see their dad. Greg had to agree. Seeing the smashed car that his father had been in the night before was painful. After they visited the car, Greg's mom took Greg and his older sister to school. His younger sister was still too upset from the hospital visit so she stayed home.

At school everyone knew about the tragic accident. No one was sure how to act around Greg. Some kids hung back and sort of stared at him. There was a mixture of pity and curiosity in their eyes. Other kids came up to Greg and just said, "I'm sorry about your dad." The majority of the boys and girls just didn't know what to do, so they said, "I'm really sorry" to Greg. Then they stayed away from him for the rest of the day. This went on for about three days and finally people started acting normal around him again. Greg and his sisters would visit their dad almost every day after school. The visits were becoming easier for Greg. He got used to his father's condition and stopped being afraid. He looked forward to the almost daily visits.

Many of Greg's family members began to come. They came to help out Greg and his sisters. He was thrilled to learn that his favorite aunt from California would be coming to his house for a while. After about five days, Greg's family had received so many flower arrangements from concerned people that their house looked like a flower shop. This didn't help Greg's younger sister's allergy to flowers. Many people also sent cards to his family. Greg's mom would take the cards into the hospital to show Greg's dad. The cards would always cheer him up.

As I said before, the visits to the hospital would usually make everyone happy. Well, one dark day, Greg's mom returned from the hospital with a mournful look in her eyes. Greg and his sisters had not gone to the hospital this time because they had been there earlier in the day. Greg's mom gathered the family together and asked them to all sit on the couch. Then she told them some shocking news. Their father had died. No one cried at first. It was almost like no one believed what they had just heard. Their mother continued to talk and told them that she was there holding his hand as he died. As she was holding his hand, he said that he saw many bright, magnificent lights. He knew he was going to heaven. He told Greg's mom that he didn't feel pain anymore and that the lights were beautiful. Then he died. By now, the news of his father's death had sunk in and a single tear rolled down Greg's face. He was sad but in a sense he was happy. His father was not in pain anymore. Greg also knew that he would always be safe. For now his dad was his guardian angel who would watch over him and protect him. His dad's love would always be with him, forever. Greg's experience helped him to realize how precious life is and that would be a lesson that would stay with him always.

The End

Before I went to bed that night, I placed David's gold wedding band in a tiny heart-shaped porcelain box next to my nightstand. The hospital had returned to me my husband's few personal effects, including his ring, when I left for my final time. The wide band was engraved on the inside with the date of our wedding, September 3, 1977, and our initials DSK/KMB. The full moon peeked through the tilted pink mini-blinds shading my bedroom window and reflected off the round piece of shiny metal. David's circle of life was now complete.

I shut my eyes and slept well that night. I was relieved that the difficult journey was over and we could begin to heal. Tomorrow I would plan my husband's funeral.

Chapter VIII

The Box

"Take me home," he whispered, and I did.

The gently sloping blacktop driveway was cold and damp under my bare feet. Even when David was alive, I routinely put on his oversized, striped terrycloth robe after a shower and walked outside to retrieve the local morning newspaper. Now it was the morning after his death. I cinched the frayed sash tightly around my thinning waist in order to shield my damp body from the frosty cold. Tiny ice crystals covered the lawn, glistening like spun sugar. The bare branches of our red maple reflected the dawn's light with its own frosty residue; gone with the season was its plush, green foliage. All that remained were the bare essentials.

At the end of my driveway lay the newspaper, haphazardly tossed from the window of an old blue station wagon along with about a hundred others to supplement a local teenager's income. I reluctantly bent down to retrieve it and slowly slipped off the thin rubber band, which secured the flimsy pages of advertisements and local news. Media attention was not something with which our family was familiar. Barely two weeks earlier, local headlines had opened our very private family life to the public: "Prominent Local Attorney Seriously Injured in One-Car Crash."

Today, the announcement was different. It wasn't on the front page; instead, it was tucked deep inside the pages, insulated from the winter morning. Retreating to my warm kitchen, I prepared my usual cup of bitter-tasting instant coffee mellowed by a generous dose of half and half. Then I cautiously opened the paper to section B, page 3—the obituaries. Still, I was startled by a familiar three-by-five, black-and-white picture positioned in the middle of the page. It was David's smiling face. He looked so happy and alive with his wide smile, and behind his glasses his laughing eyes revealed his true character. This exact picture is lovingly displayed in a delicate silver frame on Samantha's nightstand. Vestiges of goodnight kisses and tender moments of reflection smudge the glass. Another, more-crumbled version is carried daily in Richard's wallet.

My husband's youthful face was out of place with the other images on that morning's obituary page. Longevity is prevalent in Lancaster County, and David did not fit in with the octogenarians and grandmotherly images that also were smiling back at me. He didn't fit into the same category with the elderly dairy farmer and retired ninety-two-year-old seamstress; they both had passed on naturally to the next stage after long lives. David was the lone youthful figure calling out to me that morning.

It was difficult to read about my husband's life in the generous three-column article. Everything was in the past

tense. His professional memberships and accomplishments were detailed meticulously. My own name and those of his children and immediate family members looked somewhat unfamiliar in print. It was almost surreal. Normally, I would proudly cut out an article mentioning a family member's name and post it on our refrigerator with a colorful magnet. Today, I quietly closed the newspaper and hid it in a desk drawer. I still wasn't ready to face the harsh reality of David's death. I was alone at the kitchen table and embarrassed by my grief. Slowly I was accepting the reality of his passing, but the newspaper obituary had jolted me into the present with a pre-emptive strike.

Without a word about the article, I awoke the children and sent then off to school. I felt that it was important to keep their daily routine as normal as possible so that I could maintain some protective control over their lives.

I would spend a significant portion of the "day after" shopping for a container for my husband's cremated remains. I journeyed to downtown Lancaster with Mel, my husband's law partner, who kindly volunteered to meet me for my appointment with the funeral home. The three-story, stately red-brick building was just around the corner from David's first law office near the center of town. Momentarily sitting alone in my car in the parking lot, I was flooded with memories of our beginning in 1977 and his first job as an attorney. Newly married and without children, I often picked him up after work on Friday afternoons and we would go out for a modest dinner in town.

Slowly I exited from the car, leaving my happy memories behind. I was in charge of planning the final details and feeling very nervous. Mel arranged my meeting with his friend, a young partner in one of the local mortuaries. I was relieved that I did not have to research the place and only had to show up prepared to carry out my husband's wishes, which he had expressed to me a few days before.

I actually started to feel comfortable as I sat on the worn, gold brocade couch listening to soft background music. "Give your loved one a gift. Preplan your funeral," admonished a brochure on the cherry end table. We simply had not gotten around to this particular detail in our fifteen-year relationship. We were both in our forties and funerals weren't a priority. All of our attention was devoted to our young children and their vibrant and exciting lives. We did not feel like we were in the shadows of our timelines.

As I sat alone on the sofa, more memories surfaced. I recalled that David would not sign my organ donor card when I renewed my driver's license in 1979. Back then a witness signature was needed to make the status of organ donor official, but he was superstitious and did not want to sign it. Instead, Sherri, his secretary, witnessed it and signed it for me. At that time in my life I was contemplating being cremated, so this detail only seemed logical.

Therefore, it was so unexpected when David told me on his deathbed that he wanted to be cremated rather than buried. His last-minute change in philosophy took me by

surprise. I did not know of anyone who had been cremated. My few funeral experiences had been with traditional burials, so again, I had no script to follow.

We were ushered from the front parlor to an area out of public view shortly after Mel arrived. To the far side were rows of ornate display caskets lined up like cars at an auto dealership. They seemed so cumbersome and unnecessary for the physical remains of a loved one who was no longer in need of space on earth. Their plush satin liners in subtle blues and creamy whites looked inviting and comfortable, but a lifeless body would never know. We moved quickly to the collection of urns and boxes on the serious wooden shelves.

This was to be the final shopping trip for my husband. Traditionally, I was a bit frugal and I usually looked at the sales racks first for a good bargain. I didn't think that funeral homes ran clearance sales, and now was no time to pinch pennies. David deserved the best. Should I choose the rosewood box or the oak one? Oh, David always made the final decorating decisions! I was having such trouble focusing as Mel and I stood in the funeral home's morbid "showroom."

At first I just stared, not knowing what criteria to use in my selection process. I nervously remarked that one container looked like an old-fashioned bread box and that another reminded me of the genie's bottle in the 1960s TV sitcom *I Dream of Jeannie.* Mel looked at me with a perplexed expression and forced a smile while I broke the tension with a soft chuckle. I am sure that David would have approved of this light moment on such a dark day. The whole experience was so uncomfortable. I could feel perspiration penetrating my silk blouse.

"Do you have a cat or a dog?" the funeral director asked, stepping closer to us. "Perhaps you might want to consider the pet-proof model if you do," he suggested in a respectful tone.

I could just envision our cairn terrier Harry sniffing around and knocking over my husband's remains. The image didn't seem too dignified but certainly plausible; therefore, I informed him that we did, indeed, have a dog and settled on the simple, rectangular oak box, complete with the pet-proof closure. David would be safe from our curious canine in a design that was both simple and respectful.

Several days later, after the service, the senior funeral director arrived at the house with an American flag correctly folded into a triangle, the gold-trimmed guest book, several leftover programs, and...*the box*. Sam and Rick stared in wide-eyed wonderment and gleefully blurted in unison, "Dad's home!" They proceeded to flood me with inquiries: "Can he stay on the kitchen center island for cocktail hour? Can we put him in the trunk and take him to the shore this summer? Can he stay in my room some nights? What does he look like? Are his teeth in there? How did he fit in there?"

The reserved gentleman in the conservative charcoal-gray suit smiled nervously. I am sure that he was taken aback by the flurry of random questions, and I hoped that he was not offended by their candor and innocence. Their natural curiosity temporarily overshadowed their genuine sorrow, and in their own naïve ways they still were processing all of the events.

After the funeral director left, Samantha and Rick turned around and gently stroked the box's smooth oak surface. Later they told me they were grateful that they didn't have to go to a cemetery to talk to their father. Popular horror movies had created a frightening image in their young minds. Cemeteries were a scary setting for gory, macabre acts rather than a peaceful final resting place. They were relieved that their dad was not under a cold heavy stone in the damp earth, far away and surrounded by underground strangers. His warm presence was felt in the house from that day forward.

Chapter IX

The Service

"...[We] are defined by whom we have lost...," whispered Anna Quindlen's words to me through her Newsweek column, "Life After Death."

"How many people do you expect at your husband's service?" asked the woman on the phone. The church caterer was planning a luncheon in the Parish House after the 11:00 a.m. memorial service for David on Saturday, February 27th, 1993, and needed numbers. I had no idea how many people would show up to pay their respects. My own relatives were flying in from all over the country, but this was family. David's loved ones were driving up from the Philadelphia area for the day, and between the two groups, we were already well over thirty. It was difficult to select a number because I wasn't sure how many lives in our community were touched professionally and personally by my husband, so I left it to the caterer's best estimate.

Two days before the service, I met with the senior pastor of our church, The Evangelical Lutheran Church of the Holy Trinity, in downtown Lancaster. Beautifully restored, it has been a place of worship since the 1760s. David and I were kindergarten Sunday-school teachers there for seven years, and my husband was a regular usher at its early service. Pastor Lehman felt very badly that he had not gotten a chance to visit David during his stay at Jefferson Hospital. He had seen him briefly at Lancaster General and was going to make a trip to Philadelphia on the day that David died. When he came into the house, he went directly to the left set of bookshelves in the family room and scanned all of our framed pictures. He said, "David was such a family man; I am so sorry."

I gestured him to sit on the couch beside me. His eyes were moist. I was in the odd position of comforting the pastor, and I told him that David and I had managed to plan the service during his final days in the hospital. He was amazed at my husband's lucidity during this time and was pleased that the service would be to his liking. The senior minister started to take notes in a small spiral notebook as I told him of our musical selections. Since David was a retired naval officer, the "Navy Hymn" was his first choice, followed by his second favorite piece, "Amazing Grace." I was able to correctly guess both of these selections when he and I discussed the service. David was pleased that I knew him so well by coming up with the right answers.

The memorial was to be brief and uplifting. Since David had been cremated, the only visual reminder of his passing was a large arrangement of his favorite flowers on the center altar of the cavernous church. David loved his vegetables and flower gardens at home, so it was a fitting tribute.

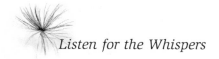

The funeral home provided a black stretch limousine to take the immediate family from Signal Hill Lane to the church. My husband's parents also rode in the limo with the children and me. The long vehicle respectfully wound down our neighborhood street, tracing David's daily workday path into the city of Lancaster past the County Court House to the church. We allowed ourselves to be enveloped by the limo's plush crimson velvet seats in silent, reverent, and nervous expectation.

My husband's eldest son, David, had spontaneously decided the night before to write and give a eulogy for his father. I was very proud of him. I knew how devastating his father's death had been to him. Young David managed to assemble the proper attire and finished it off with one of his father's neckties, which I had grabbed that morning from the hall closet. (He was going to wear one of my husband's trademark bowties, but after twenty minutes we couldn't figure out how to adjust it properly.) I was wearing my mother's gray-and-maroon wool suit, which she kindly brought from home in upstate New York. Feeling childlike, I allowed my mother to dress me, as I had not had the time to focus on my own appearance; the day before the service, we had rushed out to the mall to purchase new outfits for Samantha and Richard.

Sam and Rick had been experiencing growth spurts, so they just did not have anything appropriate to wear. The saleswoman in the department store was very helpful as Rick tried on a navy-blue blazer with shiny metal gold-like buttons. "Are you going to a wedding young man?" she politely inquired, making small talk. "No," his small voice responded, "to my Dad's funeral." The conversation abruptly ended. I paid for the jacket and we left without further explanation. These would forever be our special "Dad clothes," never to be worn again.

When we arrived at the church, the children and I were escorted by the funeral director's assistant through an unmarked outside entrance leading to the Pastor's private dressing room. This small space was separated by a thin wall behind the main altar from the large open sanctuary, which was starting to fill with mourners. It was cramped and dim, with a small crimson prayer bench and a simple wooden chair draped with the Pastor's ordinary street clothes. As we entered, he was putting on his robe and adjusting his stiff white collar. He seemed to be gathering his thoughts for the service. I spoke briefly with him.

Finally, a few moments before the service was to begin, we exited through a small wooden door framed by a narrow archway and found ourselves awash in soft organ music at the front of the church.

I was glad we did not have to enter the church from the back and walk down the main aisle, which was flanked by white pew boxes with tiny half-doors and wooden toggle latches. But when I lifted my eyes up from my feet, I was startled by the attention that was upon us. The large sanctuary was full of family, friends, and past and present students of mine. I was overcome by their presence and

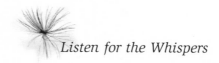

humbly settled with the children in the first pew. Norma and Dave sat directly behind us.

Next, the antique organ bellowed the "Navy Hymn" from its strong brass pipes on sentry duty in the balcony. I could feel my face start to tremble. I did not want to break down and cry already; I fought back my emotions to keep an image of strength and courage. My teeth clenched and my jaw tightened as I tried to secure my tears. The music reverberated throughout the sanctuary, reaching up into the balcony where we used to sit when we came in late for service. I know that David could hear his beloved musical choice even higher in the heavens above. Sung by the congregation, the powerful words opened the service.

> *Eternal Father, strong to save,*
> *Whose arm hath bound the restless wave,*
> *Who bidd'st the mighty ocean deep*
> *Its own appointed limits keep;*
> *Oh, hear us when we cry to Thee,*
> *For those in peril on the sea!*
>
> *O Christ! Whose voice the waters heard*
> *And hushed their raging at Thy word,*
> *Who walked'st on the foaming deep,*
> *And calm amidst its rage didst sleep;*
> *For those in peril on the sea!*
>
> *Most Holy Spirit! Who didst brood*

Upon the chaos dark and rude,
And bid its angry tumult cease,
And give, for wild confusion peace;
Oh, hear us when we cry to Thee,
For those in peril on the sea!

O Trinity of love and power!
Our brethren shield in danger's hour;
From rock and tempest, fire and foe,
Protect them wheresoe'er they go;
Thus evermore shall rise to Thee
Glad hymns of praise from land and sea.

Pastor Lehman came out of the same entrance that we just exited and slowly climbed up the small spiral staircase to the high center altar, where he would give his message. The pastor's words were heartfelt and personal as he painted a picture of a loving, spiritual family man. After another majestic organ selection, John, David's third brother, read a passage from the book of Mark. He proudly stood in front of the congregation and read one of his favorite passages in a loud, clear voice. The love for his brother came through in his words, and the pain of his loss was evident in his tone.

Next, young David gave his simple eulogy—and the floodgate of tears opened up. I could hear sobs and heavy sighs behind me from both the men and women. I was so proud of him and impressed with his composure in presenting such an emotional tribute. Here are his words:

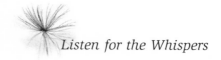

David S. Kluxen Jr. touched a variety of people during his life. His roles were that of attorney, friend, brother, son, and husband, but to Sam, Rick, and me, he was a father.

As a dad, he had a way of taking the simple things in life and making them into the most special moments. From the time I can remember, the high point of my day came usually around 6:30 in the evening when Dad would arrive home from work. We would all gather around the center island of the kitchen, chat about the day's events and eat Goldfish crackers. Whether it was throwing the Nerf football to each other in the backyard, washing the cars in the street, or making those diligent trips to Hechinger's in search of plant medicine for my dad's garden, Sam, Rick, and I will forever hold those vivid memories.

Our dad always talked to us in a tone which made us feel comfortable—he never was condescending, making him extremely approachable if any of us had a problem. He always seemed to have a peaceful disposition about himself. Even in times when stress from work got to him, he always seemed to put it all in perspective—such a level-headed person.

Over the past few years I've begun to fully realize the impact my father had on others, and the terrific role model he has been to his kids. Whenever anyone would compare me to my dad, I always felt a sense of achievement knowing that in some way I was following in his footsteps. Often I wonder how I will measure my success in life. I would be grateful to be one half the man my father was. Thanks, Dad, for being the greatest man I've ever known.

When the final hymn, "Amazing Grace," played, I could no longer hold back my own tears; they flowed freely down my face as I tried to sing the familiar words. Sam and Rick were seated on either side of me and looked up in silence as they moved closer to my trembling body. The sadness in their innocent blue eyes intensified my grief as I pulled them in closer. I never want to revisit that moment again.

The children and I appreciatively stood in the receiving line for more than two hours. Over 250 people came to say goodbye to David and it seemed like each one wanted to say a kind word to us. There were grateful former clients with compliments on his legal expertise. And the owner of the local stationery store, where David was a frequent buyer of pens and assorted gadgets, wanted to personally express her condolences—saying she would miss his frequent bright smile in her store. His fellow attorneys, both locally and from Philadelphia, had come to pay their respects to their colleague. There were some from our children's school who passed through the line that morning, and there were many who were strangers to me, but I was glad to make their acquaintance; through them, I learned a little bit more about my husband and the community's wonderful perception of him.

Why do we tend to wait to say kind words about a person until after they are gone and can't hear them? We shouldn't put off sharing our emotions and our innermost

feelings, even if they are uncomfortable. We shouldn't be afraid to bare our souls and connect with one another while we are sharing the same space here on earth. Yet we hold back, perhaps for fear of making ourselves too vulnerable and soft. Unfortunately, we sometimes make walls instead of windows. The memorial service that day reminded me that life is truly for the living, and that those moments of kindness and words of love and encouragement never go unnoticed—lingering long after we are gone. That evening I made a vow to myself to try to never let an opportunity escape without expressing the kind words that might be in my head.

Eight months after my husband's service, I was preparing to give some of his barely-worn suits to a local charity when I found in the breast pocket of one of his "church jackets" his familiar handwritten notes from a sermon on April 28, 1991—coincidentally the tenth birthday of our daughter Samantha. It was entitled, "Facing the Future Undaunted" (Romans 8:28). The scribbled words jumped out at me and seemed so relevant to the challenge that we had just faced together. "Fear needed to be replaced by trust and faith," David had written. "We know that all things work together for good for those who love God." I felt a connection to my husband's words and was comforted by his notes. I hoped that this theme had come back to him during his final and often fearful days.

Chapter X

Reaching Out

"There's no place like home…there's no place like home…," whispered Dorothy in The Wizard of Oz.

About six weeks after David died, I started receiving quite a bit of unsolicited advice from well-meaning friends and relatives who were concerned about my mental and emotional health. They suggested that I find and join a local support group for young widows. I thought that I had been coping quite well since my husband's death and was confused by their interest.

I had kept busy physically by maintaining the house and working in my yard, clearing away the dead winter leaves and twigs and turning the matted, rich soil as an invitation to springtime. I like to call this nature's aerobics. Mentally, I was challenged by my full-time job as a high school Spanish teacher—encouraging adolescents to speak another language even while their first one still needed tuning. For my emotional well being, I dedicated my remaining strength to the health and welfare of our children: Samantha and Rick at home, and David three hours away at college. The wounds were slowly healing and my active life helped me compartmentalize my grief. There was a time and a place for everything, and the structure of my days gave me a sense of normalcy.

Still shaken by my tragedy, but a pleaser by nature, I did begin scanning the local newspaper for the perfect support group. I was not sure how many young widows there were in the county. Recently, I had started keeping an eye on the local obituaries and hadn't seen any announcements about husbands who had passed in their forties. There were only folks who had died just short of the century mark.

Nevertheless, my investigation revealed a large number and variety of support groups in Lancaster County, which surprised me. There were medical support groups for various aliments, eating disorder groups, child-rearing support groups, and even pet bereavement groups. It was curious to me how we had developed into such a society that encourages reaching out to strangers for comfort and support in their most private time of need. Where were the nostalgic, loving, close-knit families whose sage advice erased the cold pain of loss over a cup of hot chocolate? Where were the soft and ample chests and open arms to run to and hide for safety?

After careful consideration and much consternation, I selected a generic bereavement group at the local community center. I used to take Sam and Rick for tot gym classes at this very same facility, which was another reason I chose it. At least the location would be familiar. Not sure of what else to do, I momentarily stopped and listened to

my whispers. It felt right.

In preparing myself for the 7:00 evening meeting, I battled over what to wear. Should I be covered from head to toe in black, the traditional mourning color, as an overt sign of my recent change in marital status? Or should I allow the emerging springtime to creep into my drab winter wardrobe? I selected a green outfit. Perhaps unconsciously, it was a symbol of a new beginning.

Lately I had felt awkward in my new role as a widow; it was as if everyone was always staring at me in pity. Perhaps it was momentary paranoia, or maybe I actually was looking for some sympathy now and then. I was very self-conscious over every move I made, as if an established governing committee of mourning officials was monitoring my actions. Each step was a new one for me, and I treaded lightly as I hesitantly ventured out alone. I certainly did not want to tarnish my dear late husband's memory in any way, but I wasn't sure what society expected of me. I wasn't able to find a directory of widowhood dos and don'ts. Well-meaning friends and neighbors didn't want to stoke the smoldering embers of my pain by asking personal questions; perhaps the stigma of the unknown made them feel uncomfortable, too. The proximity to death is an intimidating force for many.

As I entered the lobby of the community center, I immediately focused on the small cork bulletin board announcing "Bereavement Meeting Tonight, Room 10. All Welcome!" As I tried to pretend that I was casually walking down the narrow hallway, perhaps to another location, I felt the eyes of the young blonde receptionist piercing the nape of my neck. Did she know that I had lost my husband less than two months ago? Did I look sad enough? Too sad? Too happy? Should I turn around and smile at her? Once again questions and doubt flooded my head. I kept walking, concentrating on each step and wondering. I did not look back.

I was late. When David was alive I was never prompt. He would get frustrated while waiting in the car for me on Sunday mornings. We were always the last ones to be seated in the balcony section of the church. I didn't view this as the secondary seating for the stragglers, but merely rationalized that we were only closer to God. Now, since I did not have David to honk in the driveway for me to come out, I was even less punctual. Time simply was not a driving force in my life. It was a finite commodity and I was learning to accept my earthly allotment. I had learned to respect time rather than to let it be a controlling force in my life.

When I pushed open the heavy metal door and peeked in, it was evident that I was the last one to arrive for the evening's meeting. The metal folding chairs were carefully arranged in a small intimate circle. The large freshwater fish tank was filled with guppies, angelfish, and other brightly colored species swimming in their own soothing rhythm. The members of the weekly bereavement group had already taken their self-designated places in the circle.

When I had called the group leader earlier in the week, she mentioned that the first night was basically a "get acquainted" session. Then, as the months progressed, we would work through various stages of grief together.

After a cursory examination of the group, I initially felt doubtful as to whether I wanted to venture through these stages en masse. But I was learning to be patient and not to make snap judgments, so I quietly took the remaining chair next to the middle-aged female facilitator. My bottom had barely touched the hard seat when my mind began racing and my eyes started darting around the circle in a counter-clockwise direction. I guess my nervous energy needed an outlet. I could see the stained, crumpled tissues clutched in reddened, sweaty palms, and I could hear the nervous tapping of tired shoes on the vinyl floor. I speculated that this was going to be a very long hour. My tense body eased back into the cold metal chair as I tried to relax.

In a gentle voice, the group leader began by welcoming us and introducing herself. She slowly gave her credentials, and as she continued to present her resume, I continued looking around the circle, guessing each participant's circumstances.

Suddenly I snapped back to attention when I heard her say that we would go in clockwise order. Darn! This meant that I would be last! Yet it was only fitting, since I was the last one there. But I never liked being last in a group oral presentation; I performed best in a spontaneous setting.

The anticipation always made my throat dry and tight, and the rhythm of my heart became thunderous and pounded against my chest like the force of a strong wave. I was sure that people could see the undulations beneath the layers of my clothes as the blood flowed in and out of its chambers, pressing against my rib cage. I tried not to selfishly think about being last. Instead, I focused on the individuals and their sad stories.

First was an attractive, well-spoken young woman who had lost her beloved thirty-four-year-old brother two years earlier. She lovingly described him as if he was sitting right next to her. Crystal blue, her eyes lit up each time she mentioned his name and her slender, well-manicured hands fluttered about birdlike as she recounted how much fun they had had together in childhood. Her memory of him was uplifting, and hearing about their lives together, I thought of my own children's bond. But in the separation wrought by death she was unable to make the trip to the cemetery to visit him. The rows of cold headstones and ominous silence were images that she could not force herself to confront.

I nodded in agreement. I had my husband at home where the kids and I could speak to him whenever we wished, at any moment. It seemed to me that what she needed was another special place in which to remember her brother and keep his memories warm and alive. Memories can travel anywhere with us; they are intangible forces that inspire and drive our souls, I told myself.

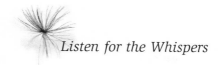

Next spoke an elderly man mourning the loss of his dear wife. He immediately started wiping the moisture from his eyes as he told of their wonderful union lasting half a century. He was lonely and broken. Never having had to cook for himself, he was learning anew how to survive.

Again, I found myself nodding in agreement. Mealtime had become difficult for me, too. I had the ability to cook, but dinnertime represented the occasion that our family gathered after a long day to trade stories, to connect with each other, and to create more memories together. It was the focal point of our days, and in order to cope, it was one of the first big adjustments I had to make after David's death. I couldn't continue the same routine without him, so we had to go forward in a new direction. We began to eat dinner earlier and without the usual cocktail hour. Somehow drinking my scotch on the rocks alone did not taste the same.

For a long time I could not bear to look at the clock on the stove and anticipate the Volvo pulling into the garage at 7:00 p.m., waiting to hear my husband's eternally cheerful voice yell, "I'm home!" The clock now ticked to the hour of seven and the house was silent. The void was so much more than I had anticipated; I had underestimated the power of our simple traditions and routines.

Fridays had become our evenings out as the children and I explored the local restaurants together. Each week we tried a new place, and after eating we would rate the food and service for fun. In the end, though, nothing could compare to the four of us around the kitchen table with a home-cooked meal. But these changes helped us to heal. Change seemed to be the key for us.

This sweet elderly man needed a positive change, too. But he didn't have the advantage of two vibrant pre-teens at home to encourage him. He was alone. I understand better now why, so often, when one mate dies after a long union that the other quickly follows. We become creatures of habit: the longer we are in our environment, the harder it is to change. While the old man continued to proclaim his love for his late wife and describe his misery without her, I hoped that he could at least connect with a senior citizen group or Meals on Wheels to nourish him.

The details of each story were different. Each experience was slightly unique yet the common bond of loneliness and hurt gradually tightened the circle. A man whose wife had died five-and-one-half years ago could not walk into the lobby of the bank where they used to go together every Friday.

Finally, my heart went out to the heavy-set woman whose daughter had overdosed on drugs and left three small children in her care. This grandmother was obviously overwhelmed by her newfound responsibility. Her problems were complex and seemingly endless.

As parents, we do the best we can with our children; we do not anticipate having to raise the next generation, too. A vital piece had been chiseled from the foundation of her life and the rest of the edifice was on the verge of

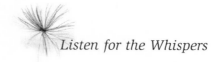

collapse. I knew what it felt like to have a family unit rearranged, and my heart ached for her loss. I could not imagine the loss of one of my children.

After the first few members of the circle had spoken, I decided that this was going to be my first and last attendance at a structured support group, and I wanted to leave behind positive thoughts and hope in a room that was suffocated by sadness. When my turn finally came, the anticipatory lump dissolved in my throat. I told the gathering of the short yet special time that David and I had together while he lay mute and paralyzed in Philadelphia. We were given the opportunity to complete our circle of life together—to look into one another's eyes and say our mortal good-byes. We knew that we would be together again someday, and that in the meantime I would care for our cherished children and keep him alive in their hearts forever.

Throughout my confession, the folded white tissue in my hands remained dry. The group leader looked at me with skepticism. How could I have come to this acceptance in six short weeks? The secret was that I was never alone. David and I passed through some of the stages of grief in those two weeks just like we did everything else in our marriage—together. We always shared and we were always connected. And now, my support group was waiting for me at home.

At the end of the meeting, I bid goodbye to each member with a warm hug and wished him or her well on the journey of recovery. I knew that some would reach the end sooner than others and perhaps one would linger on the trail forever, not being able to let go of despair.

Back in the car, I rolled down the window and let the cool night air drift across my smile and erase the memories of the past hour. The *whisper* was loud and clear. We were doing just fine. If a vessel has been properly stocked and adequately prepared, it will survive a violent storm battered and slightly damaged—but intact and ready to sail once more. I felt that we had weathered our tempest and were heading back out to the open sea together.

An hour-and-a-half later, when the garage door went up at our house on Signal Hill Lane, Samantha and Rick came into the garage. Initially they were not sure if this whole event had been such a good idea, but they respected my parental decision. To them I appeared strong and unwavering; they did not know that the outside layer was fragile and beneath it was another of insecurity. They did not see my tears washed down the drain after a hot shower or feel my body quivering with fear in my worst moments of doubt late at night.

Standing in the damp garage, I told them about the events of the evening. I told them that we were doing well as a family. At the same time, out of respect for the members of the group, I was careful to not diminish the importance of its existence. For the ones that I left behind, there was still a real need to vent their feelings in that forum and to find a new order in their lives.

The glue holding the broken pieces of my life was my

family bonds and our deep love for one another. My support came in the form of phone calls, laughter, and hugs. I didn't have to share my story with strangers to regain my strength. I was rebuilding it right here at home with my children, day by day. And for that, I felt both fortunate and grateful.

Chapter XI

The Other Side of the Bed

"I love you," I whispered each night.

His two foam pillows were cold and empty. Since David's death, the silence in our bedroom had become loud and painful. Bedtime used to be a special quiet time for us when we shared the last of the day's events as we held each other and drifted off to sleep. The children were in their nearby rooms asleep and we were just husband and wife, together, like we were in our beginning. The days always ended with a warm embrace and a *whisper*, "I love you."

I miss the *whispers*, the hugs; I don't like bedtime now and put if off way past my usual hour to avoid being alone there. I'm not sure how we originally decided, but I always slept on the left side of the bed, and David was on the right side. Because this habit was so strong, the few times David spent the night away from home I still never rolled into his space. And so for the first six months without him, I dared not move onto his side of the bed. It may sound silly, but it was almost as if it were sacred ground—that deep in the mattress I could still detect his scent. It was almost as if perhaps I was waiting for him to crawl back into bed next to me, but intellectually I knew that this was not going to happen.

During a warm August night in 1993, I was listening to

the familiar wind chime outside my bedroom window as I tried to get to sleep. I reached up to catch the late-summer breeze coming in my window. My hand slipped to the right side of the bed and rested on my husband's pillow. I didn't jerk it back like I usually did but let my arm linger there for a moment. Recently, the perpetual lump in my throat had been subsiding. My eyes were not as quick to well up with tears at the mention of David's name or the scream of an ambulance siren, and my face didn't ache from forced insincere smiles. The details of the accident were fading, although I accepted that they would never totally go away. I was growing stronger each day and stretching myself in ways that I never knew I could. I peeled the covers back from his side of the bed and let the summer air invade his memory. Although I was not totally feeling whole again, I was healing. Unlike a starfish that can regenerate a lost arm, I could never bring back my missing partner but I could still grow and repair. I need just a little more space tonight, I thought, as I smoothed the sheets in my direction.

Each night my fear lessened and I crept a little closer to the other side of the bed. The new me needed more room and I knew that I had David's approval.

With my growing confidence, I was ready to tackle the last painful piece of my ordeal. I had not removed any of David's personal articles and had hastily stowed his belongings from the office down in the basement, where I did not have to look at them. I had hidden a part of him.

In a spider-filled corner of the garage there was a white

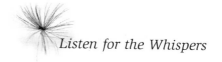

plastic bag from Lancaster General Hospital containing more personal effects. The hospital insisted that I take all of these items after he was moved to Philadelphia. In addition to his wallet, wedding ring, and watch, they gave me the torn remains of his clothing from the night of the accident. Those painful souvenirs were my reality.

Several times, when I wasn't sure if I was still in a bad dream, I opened the bag and saw his ripped dress shirt, destroyed pin-stripe suit, and scuffed loafers. Within seconds I always drew the bag's drawstring tightly shut, locking in my nightmare. But now I needed to liberate myself from these chains that were holding me back from complete healing. I had never showed anyone the bag, and in the dead of night I hid it in one of our garbage cans for the next day's pick-up. Anonymously, off it would go in the filthy container of the big green sanitation truck and finally joined the township's history at the landfill. I thought about keeping one tiny piece of the familiar fabric, but I forced myself to let go totally so that I could move forward without a crutch.

David's clothing stayed a bit longer as I gradually transferred it from our closet to the one in the guest room. I was not quite ready to do a complete cleansing and allowed myself the luxury of time to bolster my courage. Small steps on this difficult road helped. Eventually I gave away the bulk of his clothes to the Salvation Army, but kept special items for the children and myself. Favorite t-shirts were saved for the kids, and in later years they laughed when they pulled them out and proudly wore them. We all worked hard to keep his memory alive; these fabric links brought fun to the process.

Neckties, bowties, and suspenders represented David's unique sense of style, and Rick and young David shared them equally as they entered adulthood. My husband's cufflinks, assorted old-fashioned metal tie tacks, and numerous watches were saved in a special jewelry box along with his Navy ribbons and Penn Relay track medals from high school. The most special of all was his Saint Jude Thaddeus medal. When David flew in the Naval Reserves when we first were dating, he wore this small gold medal on a thin gold chain around his neck for safe passage and good luck. Although he was not Catholic, he said that way back in his family history someone was—and that was how he got it. There were enough close calls on his Naval sojourns for him to feel a sense of magic from this medal, and he never went off without it. From time to time he would wear it when we were married and I wondered what challenge he was facing. Today, the Saint Jude Thaddeus medal is passed among us as a sign of strength and good luck, and as a connection to David whenever we face our own challenges.

The other side of the bed is totally filled now as my arms and legs freely spread out across its width. David's pillows are often occupied by our dog Harry, who has taken to keeping me company at night. Harry's deep breathing and occasional snoring provide welcome breaks from the silence of my room.

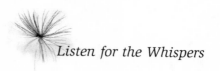

Section Three:

Details

Chapter XII

Widowhood:
It Didn't Come with Directions

"Get married again," David whispered.

After David and I married in 1977, my new washer and dryer arrived with a thick, glossy manual, complete with extensive directions in Spanish, French, and English; attached to the back of the appliances was a fancy warranty printed in Old English-style print on parchment paper protected by a clear plastic pouch. And my recently purchased lamb's wool sweater was packaged with washing instructions and tips for prolonged wear printed on a silk tab permanently sewn into the garment. However, my new marital status, widowhood, didn't come with a brochure, fancy warranties, or with any directions to guide me through the day-to-day challenges of single parenthood. Since I had already made the emotional choice to take charge of the situation as best I could, I had to gather all the courage and practical knowledge I could in order to proceed confidently and credibly.

When my husband and I built our second home, we were so excited. This was to be our dream house and our final abode. Fatefully, for David, it was. And for me, 1036 Signal Hill Lane probably would be my final home before downsizing after the last of the children graduated college. Luckily, I was always the "fix-it person" around the house, so I wasn't as intimidated as I might have been if the roles had been reversed. I could already change the flappers on the toilet, knew where the fuse box and water shut-off valves were located, and knew the difference between a Phillip's-head screwdriver and a flat-head one. I was also quite handy with power tools and especially enjoyed using the electric drill and circular sander when I refinished our dining room furniture in my younger, more energetic days.

But now, I started to listen to new sounds in the house, sounds to which I was not previously attuned. I worried more. Would the motor of the overworked sump pump make it through the rainstorm? Were those creaking and moaning sounds in the winter wind just the joists shifting in the attic or was the vinyl siding coming loose? I had lost my sounding board, so my many questions reverberated endlessly in my mind. I alone was responsible for everything in my world, and I needed to develop a true sense of my environment and trust my instincts. Otherwise, I was going to become an incurably paranoid human being.

In order to keep the house in good working order, I assembled a network of service people and handymen for repairs I could not handle myself. I had become well-versed in detailing problems over the phone. But all of my planning, preparation, and record-keeping did not provide for some emergencies.

About a week after David's death, Lancaster suffered one of its usual late-winter blasts. The day started with innocent flakes dancing down from the gray skies, giving a fresh coating to the old stained snow. Just like the top of a French pastry, it was light and fluffy and appealing to the eye. But by nightfall the light snow got heavier and started to clog the driveway and fill the gutters. I was concerned about its weight on the roof and felt a sense of relief when the wet snow turned to rain, hoping the snow would be washed away. But the night grew colder and the drizzle transformed into ice pellets firing against the windows and siding of the house like a machine gun. After tucking Samantha and Rick into bed, I just sat and stared out the French doors at the wrath of the winter storm.

A new worry consumed me when I saw layers of ice building up on the metal canister of our heat pump, and at midnight, I felt the need to take some action. I understood the workings of the heat pump well enough to know that I needed to keep the top and side vents clear for air flow and the fan blade to rotate freely. The overhang of the roof along the garage did not quite protect the unit, so I decided to build something to shelter it.

Late at night, rummaging through the garage for spare wood pieces and nails and a hammer, I irrationally started to construct a lean-to type structure around the heat pump to deflect the icy rain. By 2:00 a.m. I had completed a rudimentary barrier with two plastic trash-can lids and a wooden saw horse. I was physically exhausted, cold, and still tremendously worried about the prospect of losing heat. I knew that I had to get up and go to work in four hours and was starting to panic.

Working my way back through the garage and into the warm house, I cracked the top of my left kneecap on the metal door jam. Piercing pains radiated down my leg as I fell to the floor just inside the house. Unable to move for a moment because of my injury, tears flooded down my face and heavy sobs erupted from the pit of my stomach. I was afraid, and alone.

Pulling myself up by the edge of the kitchen counter, I stood in front of the sink and caught a glimpse of my reflection in the window. Because of my haste to go outside and fix the problem, I forgot to put a winter hat on and now my short brown hair was matted down by ice and snow. Gone was all makeup, and smudges of my mascara enhanced the deep circles under my red and swollen eyes. My lips, curling downward with deep lines, were dry and cracked. I was aghast at the image.

For one brief moment, I felt so drawn to the edge of life that I wondered if I could go on. My world seemed to be crashing in on me and I could not feel any hope. Doubt and uncertainty plagued me. If the days ahead were going to be more of the same, I didn't know how I was going to make it. And then I closed my tired eyelids and thought of Samantha and Rick innocently sleeping upstairs in their warm beds, unaware of the chaos that was threatening my sanity. I could never leave them alone as orphans in the

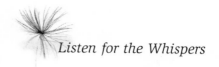

world. I was their only parent now and *had* to go on.

Bending over the sink and exhaling deeply, I asked God to please give me more strength so that I could make it through the night. I even called out to David, asking him for some sign of support since I was feeling so alone. After about ten minutes in a slumped position on the counter, that defining moment miraculously passed. With a sense of calm I removed my damp blue down parka and retreated to my bedroom. Leaving on my damp wool sweater and soggy spandex leggings, I crawled in to bed once again, wrapping the down comforter around me to insulate me from further danger.

Morning came just as it always does, and by the time I got out of the shower, the bright sunshine was generously melting away the remains of the ice on my lean-to. The primitive construct looked very silly against the white vinyl siding in the daylight; before going to work, I sheepishly disassembled it to let the heat pump totally thaw out. Reflecting upon the night's emotional test, I decided that never again would I judge anyone who may be pushed to the brink of life and, as a result of such despair, helplessly drift over. I was grateful that I was somehow given the strength to pull myself back. Slowly, my courage grew as our daily lives continued.

There were other moments that tested my fortitude. One sunny afternoon in the summer after David's death, I was cooking chicken outdoors. It was a particularly windy day, and I had positioned our small cast-iron gas grill close to the side of the house for protection. As the meat was cooking, I returned to the kitchen to prepare the rest of the meal. Dark smoke from the olive oil marinade dripping on the hot lava rocks swirled about the enclosed patio like a small tornado. The sizzling of the poultry on the metal rack blended with the classical music from the stereo. Suddenly, I heard an unfamiliar hissing sound. I casually strolled out to see if a piece of chicken had mistakenly slipped down onto the coals. Instead, a large orange flame was whipping erratically in the wind and licking dangerously close to the vinyl siding. The black rubber propane hose, normally connected to the underside of the grill, had disconnected and was now freely thrashing while spitting fire like a blowtorch.

My first instinct was to scream for help, but I was jolted back into reality when I realized that there was no one there to help me. My now thirteen-year-old daughter had just come up from the basement as I went dashing into the garage to retrieve a small fire extinguisher. Thanks to elementary school emergency checklists, we had purchased two extinguishers and kept one in the garage and one upstairs. I grabbed the device and ran back out to the patio.

First I pulled the grill away from the house and then, not exactly sure how to operate the extinguisher and not having the presence of mind to read the directions, I simply pulled out the red plastic pin and squeezed the black handles together while aiming at the flame—hoping for the best. Out came a rush of white powder, which immediately killed the fire. There was a dusty residue all over the grill, nearby

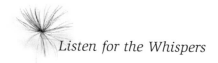

flowers, and our partially cooked dinner. In a last ditch effort to make sure everything was safe, I turned off the valve on the propane gas tank. It was then that my knees started to buckle as the reality of the situation took hold, so I sat down on the bare bricks to collect my thoughts. What had consumed a full day's energy was only a matter of moments on the clock.

Samantha had been standing inside the sunroom, watching the whole saga through the screen door. "Boy, Mom," she proudly announced, "you can even put out fires!"

I looked up at her smiling face and felt a genuine sense of satisfaction. "Yes I can!" I said. "I can do it all!" At least for this moment, I thought.

Several months later another fire emergency arose, but this time I wasn't home. Thankfully, my previous example of maintaining calm in the face of a crisis paid off. It was a crisp October Saturday morning and I had gotten up unusually early to meet a friend for breakfast, then went grocery shopping. The children were still in bed. On the way out of the house, I kissed each of their sleepy heads good-bye and left a note to tell them where I went. Their eyelids barely opened.

Three hours later I rounded the corner and drove up the gentle incline back into our development. Just around the bend on our street, a large red fire truck came into focus... then a shiny white police cruiser...and last of all an orange-and-white ambulance. My heart sank and I could feel my blood pressure drop as it always does in reaction to an emergency.

I pulled up behind the fire engine and tried to assess the situation from the front seat of my car. "Perhaps it wasn't our house," I thought out loud. But then I noticed a thick canvas hose running through my wide-open front door.

Samantha came running down from my neighbor's driveway with Harry on his red leash. She was still in her nightclothes and the two of them looked perfectly fine. "Don't worry Mom," she announced, "it's not that bad."

Not that bad!? That meant something had happened that wasn't good.

Next, my neighbor came jogging across our front lawn and assured me, "Don't worry about Rick, it's not that bad." There came those words again: *Not that bad!* But Rick was nowhere in sight, so something must have happened to him.

Finally, the fireman came to the driver's side of my car where I was still patiently sitting in an apparent state of shock. He looked me right in the eye and said, "You were lucky ma'am, it's not that bad." That was the third *Not that bad!* in less than four minutes, and I still did not know what had happened.

I forced my anxious body out from the car and walked toward the house. I felt so guilty that I was not home to pro-tect everyone. I hadn't been there when they needed me.

As the story unfolded, I learned that Samantha and Rick got up about an hour after I left and ate a leisurely breakfast in front of the television. Then Rick went back upstairs to

his room and was reading a sports magazine with the aid of a high-intensity arm lamp on the bookshelf next to his bed. It was a dark and gloomy morning, so he needed the extra light.

Several nights prior, when I was saying goodnight to him, I noticed that the screw on the arm of that same lamp had loosened, causing the head to slip downward until it hit the lamp's base. At the same time I took note of some capsule sparklers—mild legal fireworks sold at our local market—left over from the previous Fourth of July sitting nearby. I momentarily thought that perhaps that was not a good location for them, and that I would move them in the morning. But, tomorrow came and went—and my best parental intentions along with it.

Meanwhile, Sam was downstairs talking to a girlfriend on the phone as Rick went to take a shower, leaving the hot lamp illuminated. Shortly, he heard a soft crackling sound coming from his room. He peeked in to discover that one of the sparklers was spraying its white sparks in a wide arc on the bookshelf. Panicking that that incendiary would harm his goldfish, he swept it to the floor with the back of his hand and it landed on a fuzzy bedroom slipper. The slipper immediately caught fire, creating a larger flame dangerously close to his bed skirt. Instinctively, he tried to put out the fire with his damp bath towel as he called downstairs to his sister for help.

Sam promptly dialed 911 to report an emergency. (Later, she wondered if she could get a copy of the recording because she thought that she did a very good job and wanted to hear a replay.) While Rick was concerned about the property damage upstairs and tried to keep the fire contained, Samantha retrieved Harry and then went upstairs to force Rick to leave the house.

At this point there was quite a bit of acrid black smoke filling the upstairs. My children, with Harry, quickly made their way down the steps and out the front door just as the fire truck arrived. The timing of the emergency vehicles was perfect, for at this point the fire had burned through the carpet and padding and was starting to ignite the wooden sub-flooring. I don't think that the fire chief quite believed the sequence of events, but I was just glad that everyone was safe.

After the police car and fire truck left, I checked on Rick, who was sitting in the back of the ambulance with two attendants. They recommended that I take him to a doctor to treat the minor burns. When he had flicked the sparkler to the floor, the intense heat burned the top of his left hand and three fingers. We immediately got in the car and headed to the pediatrician. Rick apologized all of the way to the doctor's office and I assured him that it was an accident. I, too, was to blame for not removing the dangerous fireworks—and that malfunctioning lamp—when I first noticed them. It was a lesson learned.

When it came to household business matters, the best advice I got was from my brother-in-law Richard, Jill's

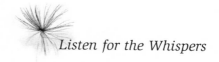

husband, who was an attorney in New York City. "Don't make any decisions for six months," he suggested. While I was anxious, after my period of mourning, to bring the tragedy of David's passing to some sort of closure, this proved to be wise advice and I was glad that I heeded it. The waters had become so muddied and unclear that I just needed time to focus.

Piles of paper covered the center island in the kitchen. Each one represented a different category and all had various due dates. The paperwork after David's death was more than I ever anticipated. I was glad that at least I had some business sense from my job as a commercial litigation paralegal, but it was still overwhelming at times. Credit cards needed to be cancelled, memberships to professional organizations suspended, and the household bills put in my name alone. Every day the mailman brought more forms that needed to be signed and notarized; sometimes a copy of the death certificate had to be attached.

There must be quite a few opportunists in the world whose primary mission is to read the obituaries, because the phone rang constantly with deals on cemetery headstones and home alarm systems. Numerous investment people were ready and willing to help me take care of my finances in case there was a big windfall.

Fortunately, trustworthy friends and family stepped in to guide me through this maze of details. My father tutored me in investment strategies, and soon I regained enough confidence to start making some of my own decisions and was able to successfully reduce my mortgage rate and re-finance my home. No longer did I want to liquidate all of my assets and run away with the children to some unknown place where we could simply live on the cash I had accumulated.

As the new head of household, I also had to adjust to being the one in charge of paying when we were out and being the driver at all times for the children. I was never one to carry a lot of cash; a couple of times I even left home without money and had to return to retrieve it. Often, I secretly counted my money under the table to make sure I had enough and carried a tip card so I didn't have to think about the math. I also decided to limit myself to one drink at dinner, since I was always the designated driver. If we left the house in daylight, I had to think about carrying my regular glasses along with my prescription sunglasses for a possible trip home in the dark. These adjustments were minor but ones that had to be made.

Next to business affairs, the biggest adjustment was my social status. The first time that I went out socially was a year after David's death, when some friends insisted that I go with them to a spring get-together at a private club in Lancaster. I dragged my feet at first and was hesitant to leave the kids home alone, but they insisted that it was time for me to have some fun. They arranged to pick me up, and the whole time that I sat in the back seat of their BMW, I felt like the third wheel at the prom. That night I learned that it is hard to mingle when you are newly single—especially

when you had neither intended nor wanted to be.

After arriving, we casually talked to some acquaintances and then my friends were pulled off into a conversation that did not include me. So I went to the bar in the corner of the large ballroom and, seating myself near a row of rowdy men, ordered my own drink: "J&B on the rocks with a twist, please." As couples laughed and danced on the wooden floor, I made numerous trips to the ladies room to check on the kids via cell phone. I was working very hard at appearing happy, but that night I felt like the world was for couples only and I didn't fit in. Finally, after one enormously long hour, I couldn't fake it anymore. I found my friend's husband in the crowded room and politely asked him to take me home. Perhaps it was just not the right time or the right place to get back into a social setting. I still felt vulnerable and very conspicuous. Basically, I didn't know how to be single after fifteen years of marriage.

It actually took me two years to figure out who I was and how to handle my new status as a young widow. I promised my children that I would not hang out in singles bars and drink fancy drinks and smoke cigarettes. This was easy because I never smoked and Lancaster was not exactly a hotbed of hopping night spots for "cougars." I didn't relish the idea of being a dating role model for my adolescent children and wanted to make sure that they did not feel slighted by my personal desires. It was difficult to trust that I could be happy again.

That said, I was not burdened by any guilt of entering

into another relationship, because in his final days, David gave me the gift of his permission by *whispering*, "Get married again."

At the time, I was appalled at the thought of having another man in my life, but wisely he knew that I was young and had too much love to offer to live alone for the rest of my days. The children would grow up and eventually move away, and I might again want or need to share my life with someone.

Oddly enough, my old college boyfriend circled back into my life after an absence of fourteen years. He was truly saddened by my circumstances and was single himself after his recent divorce. Although it was fun to reconnect, and falling back into comfortable arms felt good, the timing was not right. One of the most difficult things I ever did was to say no when he asked me to marry him after dating for about a year. I was feeling stronger each month, but there was still plenty of healing for the children and myself. It would have been selfish of me to indulge my desires before completing my family's recovery. I knew the investment of time and understanding would come back to me one-hundred-dred-fold as I saw my children grow and thrive. I did worry that another opportunity would never come again, but I stayed the course.

Chapter XIII

The Ring

"… till death do we part," I whispered at the altar.

Size 7 1/2. The one-inch wide gold ring fit securely in the delicate floral-print porcelain container on the nightstand in my bedroom. My husband's wedding band had been lovingly stored for safekeeping after his untimely death. Each night when I went to bed, I glanced at the heart-shaped container and wondered what I should do with this leftover symbol of our love and commitment to one another.

Finally, it came to me!

I took the gold ring from its protective china case to a jewelry shop in the local mall. I explained to the elderly goldsmith that I wanted to divide the ring into two equal, separate rings. There would be one for Samantha and one for Richard. I briefly and tearfully told him what had happened to my husband and how I wanted to share this token of our union with our children. I wanted to give them a tangible reminder of their parentage and the love that brought them into the world.

On April 28, 1999, Samantha's eighteenth birthday, I presented my daughter with her half of the gold wedding band and explained my intentions. With a broad, innocent smile consuming her face, she cradled the piece of gold in her delicate hands. Bursting with enthusiasm, she asked if she could have the ring engraved. Several days later I returned with her to the jewelry shop, where once again I met with the goldsmith. He quickly measured her ring size and asked her what she wanted to have engraved inside the band.

"Oh, that's easy," she said cheerfully. "Daddy's Girl."

A sudden, intense wave of latent sorrow swept over me like a tsunami. I was not prepared for my daughter's child-like response. Embarrassed by my public display of emotion, I tried quickly to wipe the tears from my blushing face and forced a smile to my trembling lips. Samantha gently wrapped her long, thin arms around me as if she was spinning a cocoon to insulate me from melancholy.

"What else would I have put?" she said, her own eyes brimming.

"But of course," I murmured. "I should have known."

Two years later, Richard and I made the same journey to the familiar jewelry store. The identical scenario was replayed at the front glass counter. I tried to anticipate my son's response to the engraving question so as to avoid another potentially embarrassing moment in the mall. Since his father's death, Rick had grown to become the man in the house and I could feel his protective shield around me. Now he calmly and precisely explained that he wanted his own initials and his father's initials—separated by a dash and followed by the date of his eighteenth birthday, January 4,

2001—on the inside of the ring. They would forever be linked in a circle of gold.

Today, two identical half-inch-wide gold bands fit snugly on Samantha's and Richard's right hands. When the three of us are together, my eyes are drawn to these shiny circles of love. For me, the rings are bold, bittersweet reminders of my life as a wife for fifteen years and a future cut short by a tragic accident. For my children, these priceless bands represent their family legacy and are daily visual reminders of their father's love and devotion.

A band of gold had been physically divided into two separate pieces, but spiritually, it linked the four of us as one.

Chapter XIV

A New Beginning

Every night I whisper to God, "Thank you. I have truly been blessed by so many gifts."

One Saturday morning in early July 2007, my daughter Samantha asked me, "Hey, Mom...what's going on with your book? Why haven't you finished it yet?" I stood at the foot of the stairs and looked into her face. Bright, inquisitive, and extremely perceptive, she was no longer a child but was married and a first-year practicing attorney in a suburban Philadelphia law firm.

I was caught off-guard by her question and fumbled for a response. Finally, after reflecting on her inquiry I had to honestly respond, "I don't know." And so the next day I dug out all of the writing that I had started at the beginning of my journey and vowed to finish it by that August. It was painful to go back and read my words, which described my feelings and the events that took me down a path of grief. I couldn't believe that I had written so much and was glad that I had carefully documented the details that were now somewhat fuzzy in my memory. I was ready to write the final chapters now, thanks to the prodding of my daughter, and for the next three weeks I sat in the warm summer sun and once again wrote, cried, and remembered.

So much has happened since I penned my first chapters. We have all been successful so far in our journey and continue to do well.

Young David graduated from Penn State in 1994 with a business degree. He is successfully employed in the insurance field and lives in Dallas, Texas. Unfortunately his mother died after a courageous battle with cancer in 2005, and as a result his bond with Samantha, Rick, and me is stronger than ever.

Samantha graduated from Franklin and Marshall College in Lancaster in 2003 with a political science degree and completed graduate work at Villanova Law School in 2006. She specializes in health care law in suburban Philadelphia. In August 2004, she and her high school sweetheart, Craig LaBarbera, an elementary school teacher, were married in Lancaster. Her stepbrother David walked her down the aisle, and her brother Rick toasted the newlyweds and twirled his newly married sister on the dance floor for her first dance. When Samantha walked down the aisle at Saint Mary's church, I could see her father's ring on her right hand and I knew that he was walking down the aisle with her on that special day.

In 2005, Rick graduated from Villanova University as a finance major and now lives in Hoboken, New Jersey. He commutes into New York City where he works in the advertising industry.

David, Samantha, and Rick continued to be a focus of

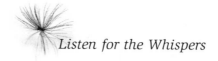

joy in my own life. It was bittersweet to see my children mature and leave the nest, and while I am so proud of their accomplishments and their courage, I am saddened by the fact that there will always be a missing piece in their lives.

In November 2003, I said good-bye to my loyal companion Harry. We had sixteen wonderful years of walks and secrets together. After I took him on his final ride to the vet, I traveled to a local restaurant and made a farewell toast to Harry with a Tanqueray (our dog's middle name given by David) Gin martini—double olives, of course.

David's parents, Norma and Dave, are still living independently in the home where they raised all of their boys in Fort Washington, Pennsylvania. Their three surviving sons—Bob, John, and Tom—all live nearby, watching over them and lending them a hand when needed.

My parents, Marjorie and Richard Burgess, continue to live during the summer months in their home of 59 years in Ames, New York, and spend the cooler months at their home on Marco Island, Florida.

My sisters—Christine, Jill, and Vanessa—continue to encourage me, as does our "fifth sister" Kathy, who is now married and has a son and a daughter of her own in Palo Alto, California.

In the spring of 2002, Samantha and Craig set me up on a blind date with Thomas W. Meredith Jr., the father of two grown sons, Tommy and Jonathan. They urged me to move on with my life and enjoy myself. On April 10, 2004, Tom and I were married in New York City at Tavern on the Green.

That summer I sold my home at 1036 Signal Hill Lane and moved up the street to share a new home with Tom.

It was difficult to sell my home with all of its memories and reminders, but Tom deserved a neutral base on which to begin our new existence. He has been generous with my children and respectful of their father's memory. Shortly after we met, he expressed his concern about competing with David's legacy, and I tried to explain that I had plenty of room for new memories and plenty of love to give him. My past will always exist and I know that David wanted me to have this new future. I hope this story will help Tom to better understand the person I was—and the person I am today.

I am still teaching Spanish at Hempfield High School and will continue doing so as long as it remains as enjoyable and rewarding as it has been for over twenty years. And now Tom and I have entered the next stage of life together— grandparenthood! We joyfully welcomed the birth of Max David LaBarbera on July 21, 2008.

The circle of life continues into the next generation.

Chapter XV

Sunlight

Throughout my personal journey following David's passing, I learned so much about my family, my children, myself... Perhaps a small part of me needed to die in order for the rest of me to live more richly.

My vision has slowly come into new focus. The lenses through which I previously viewed the world have changed: no longer are they tinted by a feeling of false self-importance or narrow-minded goals. Each of us is but a small speck in a giant universe.

My ears now hear sounds that were previously on another frequency. I try to filter out the other distracting, insignificant reverberations and strain to hear their true essence. They are whispers, not booming shouts. These simple yet powerful messages remind me that I am not alone in this world.

My former unrealistic, unyielding grasp on life has dissolved. It has been replaced by a comforting and gentle embrace, which admits positive experiences and allows me to let go of destructive ones. I am no longer afraid that if I lose my grip on temporary earthly treasures, I will end up poorer.

The source of my true wealth and happiness is that of love. Pure love never tarnishes or disappears; it only grows greater and stronger if we continue to nurture it. In the end, joy, love's by-product, will adorn our hours and enrich our days.

So now I try my best to listen only to my renewed, loving heart and forgiving soul. Moments of angst and indecision are saved for routine daily chores. My authentic being is guided by my special *whispers.* I respect their quiet strength and consider myself lucky to have been introduced to them.

I have been forced to look directly into the face of death and, curiously enough, it smiled back at me and reassured me that it is a natural part of the circle of life. I am no longer as fearful of my own mortality or the mortality of those I love deeply. I feel liberated to enjoy my life's journey and to explore the universe during the time that I am allowed. I am free to be me.

Part II

G-R-I-E-F:
A Spelling Lesson

Part II

G-R-I-E-F:
A Spelling Lesson

G is for grounded. *Believe in your "little voice" and let it guide you to your "bigger voice."*

Fear can be debilitating. It distorts the image of our true self and cripples our ability to walk freely on life's path. When the balance of our lives is disrupted, we lose the hard-earned trust in ourselves. In an act of desperation, we are tempted to hand the controls over to well-meaning friends and family members.

After my husband's funeral, I needed to strengthen my own "little voice"—to listen to my *whispers* and trust them to guide me through my anxious moments. By believing in myself, I learned to be more patient and to allow my instincts to be my rudder. I tried not to instantly react to a situation but instead modulate my responses. I worked diligently to think through my emotions in a deliberate and thoughtful manner. I heard the advice of others, but in the end I listened to my "little voice" until it grew stronger and became my "bigger voice." It was an uneasy, unnatural feeling at first, but later it became the source of my inner peace.

"Smooth seas do not make for skillful sailors," goes the African proverb. Now, looking back, I can appreciate this as I examine the rebuilding of my inner self. Daily I began to feel stronger and noticed a difference in myself. With this newly forced self-knowledge I was becoming more empowered, and my personal boundaries—to my delight—expanded far beyond my expectations. I was healing.

Lifeline Suggestions

- Do not make any major personal or financial decisions for at least six months.

- Move very slowly but deliberately. Rome wasn't built in a day.

- Learn to ask questions again. This is not a sign of weakness but may lead you to a new source of strength.

- Listen carefully to answers.

- Don't be afraid to ask others for help while you are in your "little voice" stage. You can repay favors later.

- People often want to help, but they do not want to insult you. Take the lead and allow yourself to be helped.

- Stay away from people who say, "I know how you

feel," unless they have experienced a similar loss. Sometimes a weakened person likes to draw another vulnerable person into his or her own personal crisis thinking that misery loves company.

- Don't rely upon your children for strength. Seek out trusted adults.

- Take long walks alone at dusk (or with a pet if you have one) and see if you can hear the *whispers*.

- Establish a different daily routine if possible.

- Embrace change.

- Today's misery can be tomorrow's comfort.

- Talk often to your loved one, either out loud or through thought, and share your feelings with him or her. This will help to validate your emotions and put them in a new order.

- Give credence to your loss. Talk about it freely.

- Don't make your loved one bigger in death than in life. Don't elevate him or her to sainthood.

- Don't be offended by people who do not perpetuate your loss. They have not necessarily forgotten; they are just living their own daily lives as we all have to do.

- Accept that some people "just don't get it" and be

thankful for your own gift of awareness.

- Dead people don't age. They are forever in our memories as they left us, so don't get upset as you move through life without them.

- Nostalgia is a warm and safe place. Take some special photos of your loved one and hug them tightly. Put a few special pictures near your bed to watch over you.

- Be careful not to linger in the past too long or too often. You need to move forward in order to stay healthy.

- Let your tears out forcefully and often in the shower so that they can be washed down the drain, freeing space in your heart for joy.

- Nothing worthwhile stays the same. Life is motion.

- Make a list of your pre-loss personal strengths. Examine them carefully with your new vision. If you have unknowingly given any up, reclaim them.

- If you can, give control of the big picture of your life to a higher source. Lighten your load, relax a little, and enjoy the details.

- Reconnect with old friends. These secondary safety nets can bolster your confidence and catch you when you falter.

- Smile at least once every day.

- Celebrate you next birthday with vigor.

R is for re-building. *Start your own construction project.*

I was so scared after my husband died. I felt like a fawn in the headlights—darting from one corner to another seeking shelter and avoiding future danger. I was afraid for my personal safety and financial prospects. I doubted my ability to be the sole provider for my family, and I was insecure about directing the formative years of my young children. Fear is not a healthy motivating force. I had lost my sounding board and was not confident in my new single status. I was reluctant to make the smallest decisions, just wanting to escape from my new reality.

I rapidly realized that the power of my grief unfortunately did not stop life. The world carried on with business as usual, oblivious to my pain. Bills were due. Decisions had to be made daily—and I was the only one there to make them. The days and months slowly marched on. Holidays, birthdays, and celebratory events cruelly continued.

My husband and I were partners in our marriage: We shared the household responsibilities and all decisions. I kept the checkbook and he made the investments. I took care of the house while he mowed the lawn and tended the vegetable garden. We each parented our son and daughter in our own styles and capitalized on our strengths. Like a brightly painted wooden see-saw in a schoolyard playground, our union was one of balance. But my side of the apparatus came crashing down when his position was vacated. Sure, I knew I could learn to fill in the gaps, but I was stunned and reluctant to venture out alone. As the calendar pages turned, I became physically and mentally tired of "doing it all." I started to resent the word *partner* because I did not have one. The word *husband* was always preceded by the word *late*, and the combination left a bitter taste on my tongue. I was constantly on the verge of tears.

For the sake of my children, I knew I couldn't go on like this. I had to temporarily put aside my emotions in order to clear my head and attempt to realign and control my life. So I turned to a safe childhood memory to ease the pain. When I was young, I enjoyed observing my father in the cramped office of his construction business. Surrounded by rumpled rolls of blueprints, I watched in wonderment as he began to create a building on paper at his elevated drawing table with a simple T-square and a worn mechanical pencil. He patiently explained to me that the foundation was a structure's strength as he carefully drew. In the end, the various layers of his drawing magically represented an entire building, complete with multi-dimensional perspectives from the inside to the outside.

Thinking of this process and his advice, I worked to look objectively at my post-trauma personal foundation. I

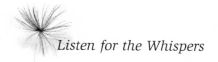

deduced that my well-placed blocks had just been slightly shifted but were still intact. Layer by layer, I needed to realign them and continue building up—trying not to be overwhelmed by whatever lay ahead. This took patience and practice at first, as I frequently had to talk myself away from the edge of resignation. Newly widowed and feeling slightly paranoid, I did not want to give the impression of incompetence or failure, so my initial "to do list" was over-ly ambitious. My false pride had nudged me to master too much too soon. This urgency led me to personal frustration and moments of unhealthy self-rejection. As a result, I learned to scale back and be more realistic. I started to rebuild once again on firmer, more positive ground with more realistic timetables. I kept in mind that I needed not only to erect strong walls for my protection and safety, but to take the time to put in some windows, too, allowing myself the future opportunity to enjoy the view of my progress. I needed to be careful not to be intimidated by the world, for some day it would be beautiful and friendly again.

Now *you* need to design your own blueprints for a real-istic self-building project. Create a pace that will allow for progress while not adding to your current frustration level. You have probably realized that life is different for you now, and by starting with some short-term goals, you can build your new healthy future. Step away from time to time in order to monitor your progress. Don't be tempted to be an over-achiever like I was. It can result in burnout and a slow-er progress.

Clear away the rubble and fallout of your tragedy and examine your foundation. Your life has probably never before been so intensely scrutinized by yourself and others. You may feel that you are under the microscope, and at first you might be put off by this. Every move, reaction, and detail has been magnified. You are one, not two. Being in charge can be lonely but as we improve, we are empowered. Try not to focus on your loss, but slowly bolster yourself and rebuild your confidence. Be patient and allow for mistakes along the way. Remember, you only lose this job by firing yourself.

Lifeline Suggestions

- Get organized and start a filing system for easy access to your new knowledge. It can be a steep learning curve and you can't be expected to remember everything at once.

- Educate yourself about your home. Know where the sources of power and water are and how to turn them off in an emergency.

- Collect a list of trustworthy service people to help you with potential problems that are beyond your expertise.

- Read all of your mail carefully—especially the fine print.

- Understand all of your bills and all of their conditions.

- Change the name on all necessary paperwork from a joint one to your single one.

- If you are concerned about privacy and personal safety, change your phone listing to a first name initial or an unlisted number. Consider a security system or adopt a dog to feel more secure.

- Get caller ID and screen your calls. Unscrupulous sales people read obituaries and can invade your personal space.

- Enroll in a personal finance course at your local community college or continuing education center. In addition, ask a trusted friend or relative to help you start to understand the ramifications of your financial future.

- See a lawyer and change your will, or make one if you don't have one. Since your life conditions have changed, so have your provisions for death.

- Make a living will. Let your wishes be known and avoid leaving it to someone else to make difficult decisions in a time of crisis.

- Hire an accountant when filing your next income tax return. Your change in status may result in different filings that may be to your economic benefit.

- Continue to ask questions. The more you ask, the more you know.

- Don't put up walls that you may have to climb over later.

- Brace yourself for the speed bumps. Annual milestones sometimes take you two steps back and only one step forward.

- Be prepared to share your story frequently in the early days of your loss. You will learn to abbreviate it in a sensitive way.

- Customize your environment. Move some furniture around and do a little redecorating when you are ready.

- Open your heart for a new season.

I is for Inspiration: *Innocent eyes are watching.*

If we are lucky enough to become parents, we hope to influence our children in a positive manner as we nurture and guide them. We do not necessarily aspire to the lofty goal of a source of inspiration for our children, although sometimes we are.

The past years' milestones had been exceptionally challenging. Every special event ignited powerful family memories and highlighted our loss. From the celebration of a high

school prom and special teenage birthdays to the passing of a driver's test, I tried to maintain a sense of joy while tempering my ever-present grief as I played the role of both parents.

Mother's Day had always been my special day. In the early years of our parenting experiences, my husband helped our young son and daughter prepare an annual special breakfast to be served to me in bed. I happily listened to the cacophony and confusion below in the kitchen and smiled to myself in anticipation of my room service. Glue-laden handmade cards adorned the bamboo tray, which was crowded with runny eggs, burnt toast, and cold coffee. After David's death, Mother's Day turned into a bittersweet occasion as I mourned the loss of the man who made me a mother.

On this particular holiday in 1997, I saw the power and significance of my new role. So I stepped out of the shadow of grief and self-pity and strolled into the uncomfortable spotlight of inspiration. Four years had gone by since the death of my daughter Samantha's father, and now at age sixteen, she had secretly entered a writing contest in the local newspaper. The Sunday edition was preparing a feature on Mother's Day and the winning entry of each age group was to be published in the special insert. When the surprise phone call came a week before publication informing us of her selection, I was stunned and filled with pride.

Here is her cherished winning entry:

Mom was the only mother to attend the Boy Scout meetings. She had no choice because a few years ago we lost my father. Suddenly, Mom entered the frightening world of single motherhood. Throughout everything she remained strong and courageous. She inspired me.

Today, Mom continues to amaze me. Her sparkling personality sets her apart from everyone. Mom has taught me what it means to be a strong, successful woman. I only hope one day I can be just like her. The greatest compliment I've ever received was being told, "You're exactly like your mom!" I hope it is true.

Little eyes were watching me, and bigger eyes continue to observe me today.

While in your self-reflective, solitary state, you may not always feel the gaze of your dependent loved ones. But furtive glances are reading your expressions as you retell your story. Your children are looking to you for strength and guidance as they rebuild their simple lives on their own elementary levels. Trust the wisdom and knowledge of your family unit as you inspire its existence with love, understanding, and experience.

Lifeline Suggestions

- You may be a source of inspiration just by your physical presence and your changed role in the family. Try to be more aware of this change and put your best foot forward.

- As your children grow up, share with them some of your own special life experiences. Offer an anchor for their young, turbulent lives.

- Plant seeds of happiness for future growth in another season.

- Speak up more and let your voice be heard.

- Be an active advocate for your family.

- Get involved in your community. Cultivate your leadership skills.

- Try and do more family things together. Create new memories.

- Try going out to dinner on Friday nights (it does not need to be fancy) and share the events of your week. Heal together.

- Stay current with the timelines of your children. Theirs change faster than yours.

- Keep your family life connections strong and healthy.

- Maintain your physical appearance as well. Looks can be inspirational, too.

- Act with a sense of confidence.

- Encourage yourself to be positive.

- Don't give out random unsolicited advice. Instead, speak up in a supportive manner when you are asked for it. Sometimes less is more.

- Admit your mistakes freely. Don't try to be perfect. Some of our best lessons come from our errors.

- Say "I love you" out loud at least once a day to your loved ones.

- Pass on family treasures and traditions. They are the inspirational underpinnings of our lives.

- *Inspiration – The act or power of moving the intellect or emotions.* (The New Merriam-Webster Dictionary)

E is for Energize: *Plug back into life on a different current.*

I now understand how much energy grief burns. In the weeks following my husband's funeral, I was mentally, physically, and emotionally exhausted. It was not until I saw a picture of myself a few weeks later that I realized its toll. I had lost over fifteen pounds (down to 110) and noticed that my clothes hung on me like rags on a scarecrow. Clumps of my thinning brown hair wound up in the drain after a shower and my appetite was that of a sparrow. My once-rosy plump cheeks were now yellowish, sallow, and very unap-

pealing. The artificial pink powder blush just sat on the surface of my pronounced cheek bones, giving the appearance of a lifeless department store mannequin. Stress, the byproduct of my grief, was obviously taking control and I needed to make a conscious decision to rein it in.

It was time to start working on the outer healing process. Already focused on developing my inner strength, I knew it was time to strengthen my body, too. I forced myself to eat more healthy portions—including lots of nutritious foods, many of which I purchased from the bounty of roadside farmer's stands in Lancaster County. I frequently snacked on fruits and vegetables and threw in an occasional glazed donut. I never did let go of my chocolate addiction, so I kept popping the M&Ms faster than usual, sometimes filling my cheeks like a hamster.

Then came the need for exercise. I understood that the body's natural endorphins are released by physical exertion, so I enrolled in a bi-weekly aerobic dance class at a local studio. Since I enjoyed music but was not naturally athletic, I found great satisfaction by freely dancing around the local gym to oldies music with other women my age, knowing that I was exercising at the same time. I could feel my battery recharging with each session and when I exited the class, I felt like a professional dancer leaving her rehearsal hall after a successful practice. In turn, my appetite increased and the additional calories began to round out my thin silhouette.

Soon a new, shorter haircut made me feel perkier and the shower drain wasn't as clogged each morning from stray tangled locks. A trip to the shopping mall for some new spring fashions shoved the old winter wardrobe to the back of my closet. A brightness and familiar glow began to illuminate my appearance again.

This was my personal experience. But it's important to get to know and understand yourself, and then determine how far you can be pushed into something new. Be careful not to go overboard and toss everything away in trying to reinvent yourself. That might be misinterpreted as a mid-life crisis, and people will start to talk. But spice up your life a little and make yourself a priority. Don't be the selfless one to take the burnt toast—as mothers often do. Step to the front of the line with purpose and pride. Remember, the by-product of our pain is our strength.

Lifeline Suggestions

- Surround yourself with positive people. You will pick up on their energy.

- Take a day to unplug from your grief. Try and liberate yourself from your burden and find energy and joy in a simple activity.

- Go to a light-hearted movie and get popcorn with lots of warm butter.

- Take a trip to the zoo with a child and watch them laugh at the monkeys.

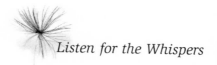

- Try a new physical activity, but don't buy all of the equipment until you are fully committed.

- Treat yourself to something special: some expensive candy, some new perfume, or a new pair of funky shoes. Show yourself that you *care* about yourself— and that you are moving forward.

- Now is not the time to be a martyr. There are no medals given out for martyrdom, and besides, no one is keeping track. Remember, Joan of Arc burned at the stake.

- Sing with the radio when you are in the car or alone at home.

- Try switching your lipstick to a more vibrant color. Or at least start wearing lipstick, even if you aren't going out. Lipstick is fine with pajamas.

- Start taking vitamins. Sometimes our bodies need an additional supplement.

- Get up a little bit earlier in the summer and enjoy the morning. Then take a "siesta" in the afternoon.

- Buy a hammock and read outside while listening to the sounds of nature.

- Treat yourself to a weekly bunch of fresh-cut flowers from your local grocery store. You can be your own secret admirer.

- Check out age-appropriate health tips in magazines at the doctor's office and hairdresser's.

- Channel all of your energy forward. Don't waste it looking back.

- Travel to and explore some new destinations with family or friends. You don't need to go far. Rediscover your own backyard.

- Start packing your life suitcase with vibrant souvenirs. Later, when you are not able to travel as much, it will be much more enjoyable unpacking it and reminiscing.

- Smile at strangers. Everyone is looking for fun.

- Share your newfound energy.

F is for fun: *"Laugh often"*

(Tim Russert—2006 Women's Conference)

I had been experiencing a misguided need to stifle my sense of humor after becoming a widow. Still feeling like I was under the social microscope, I was worried that others would view me as irreverent and disrespectful to my late husband's memory—so I artificially toned down my usual liveliness and sense of fun. Life had already become quite serious for me with its new challenges, but now I was adding to the darkness by dampening my naturally buoyant

spirit. Fortunately, I was living with two young kids who had not lost their childish ways in the wake of our tragedy. Their innocence was instrumental in guiding me back into the sunshine of my own existence.

Life provides us with an abundance of seemingly insignificant giggles. But when they are gathered all together, they can resound in one big hearty outburst. I needed to appreciate once again these small snippets of humor and stockpile them in anticipation of a vigorous roar. Laughter had always been present in our house and it needed to return again to lift my spirits.

At first we started to laugh at ourselves. My son and I laughed together at our first entry in the Boy Scout Pine Box Derby. Our crude, hand-carved car was not exactly on par with the entries of sons and dads who had access to sophisticated power tools and engineering backgrounds. But our creative use of his father's rusted lead fishing weights, drilled into the undercarriage of the chassis, gave the necessary added momentum to our creation and made us smile as it rolled lazily down the ramp in the elementary school gym. We later observed that all of the seasoned scouts had applied thin strips of metal to the tops of their wooden cars, resulting in the same outcome but with a more sophisticated appearance. We simultaneously laughed at our naiveté and ingenuity.

During my first solo winter, during a crippling snowstorm, I let myself relax after two hours of shoveling and commiserated with my next-door neighbor. At his urging, the two of us sat atop a snow bank and uncharacteristically indulged in a cold beer at eleven in the morning as we smiled at the huge white mounds that we had piled up. We laughed together at how minimal our progress had actually been during the morning hours, and when we saw a passing truck with a front-end plow, we quickly flagged it down to finish the job.

In the summer of 1993, the children and I took a three-week trip to Germany and Austria for a change of scenery and to visit some relatives. It turned out to be the opportunity for many special humorous moments as the three of us tried to blend into a foreign country with zero knowledge of the language. Together we threw off the mantle of our grief and felt the vibrant sensation of laughter ripple freely through our bodies. Spending the nights in cramped provincial inns without the familiar distraction of television, we bonded anew—creating our own nightly entertainment by taking turns washing our underwear in the bidet and sleeping on fragile beds in the tiny room. Experiencing our first nude beach on the North Sea was a family moment that will never be forgotten. As we strolled down the shoreline in our protective American bathing suits, we were confronted by an international skin parade of all shapes and sizes. Our social experience in this situation was zero: we anxiously looked to one another for confirmation of a culturally sensitive reaction. Coming up short, we collectively tossed our social restraint into the surf—giggling discreetly at each passing body. The laughter was returning to our lives. And it stayed.

Reignite the spark of your sense of humor if the flame has been snuffed out. Reintroduce yourself to the lighter side of life and balance your grief. Don't feel guilty by bringing pleasure back into your days. You deserve it. The loss will remain with you forever, but you cannot let it control you. The memory of your special relationship will never be lost and it will always occupy a very special place in your heart. Surround and insulate it with laughter and joy.

Lifeline Suggestions

- Try to find something funny in the ordinary; it is always there.

- Watch funny shows or movies with someone else. When one person starts to laugh, it is infectious.

- Don't take yourself too seriously. Life is too short and there are no "do-overs."

- Happy people attract other happy people. Try and be the magnet.

- Laugh at yourself often and out loud. You are probably quite funny.

- Go to the circus when it comes to town and rediscover the child in yourself. Ride the elephant.

- In the winter, if you can, go sledding or ice skating. Return home for hot chocolate topped with those tiny marshmallows.

- Pay for fun if you have to. Go to a zoo, water park, or theme park.

- Write a funny note on the bathroom mirror with eyeliner to a family member.

- Linger in the humor section of the card store even if you don't buy one. Laughs are free.

- Watch television channels like Comedy Central and learn some new jokes. Break them out at your next family gathering.

- Catch some old episodes of *The Three Stooges*. Who doesn't love some old-fashioned slapstick? You don't have to think or look for deep meaning. A pie in the face or a frog down the back of an evening gown is always funny.

- Life is to be enjoyed, not just endured. You've already rented the space, so make the most of it!

- Look at your smile in the mirror. It is beautiful.

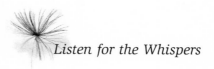

Part III

Your Healing

Journal

Now it is your turn to write...

MONTH #1 "When one door of happiness closes, another opens, but often we look so long at the closed door that we do not see the one that has been opened for us." (Helen Keller)

_____
_____
_____
_____
_____
_____
_____
_____
_____
_____
_____
_____
_____
_____
_____
_____
_____
_____
_____
_____
_____
_____

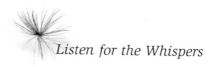

MONTH #2 "Perhaps there are not stars in the sky, but rather openings where our loved ones shined down to let us know they are happy." (Eskimo proverb)

MONTH #3 "Joy and sorrow are next-door neighbors." (Proverb)

MONTH #4 "That which does not kill you makes you stronger." (Nietzsche)

MONTH #5 "Healing from grief is not the process of forgetting. It is the process of remembering with less pain and more joy." (Author unknown)

_____

_____

_____

_____

_____

_____

_____

_____

_____

_____

_____

_____

_____

_____

_____

_____

_____

_____

_____

_____

_____

_____

_____

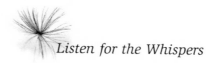

MONTH #6 "Life is like riding a bicycle. You don't fall off unless you stop pedaling." (Anonymous)

MONTH #7 "Hope is grief's best music." (Proverb)

MONTH #8 "Heed the still small voice that so seldom leads us wrong, and never into folly." (Marquise du Deffand)

MONTH #9 "No one would ever have crossed the ocean if he could have gotten off the ship in a storm." (Charles F. Kettering)

_____
_____
_____
_____
_____
_____
_____
_____
_____
_____
_____
_____
_____
_____
_____
_____
_____
_____
_____
_____
_____
_____

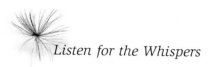

MONTH #10 "Life is not separate from death. It only looks that way." (Native American Proverb)

_____

_____

_____

_____

_____

_____

_____

_____

_____

_____

_____

_____

_____

_____

_____

_____

_____

_____

_____

_____

_____

_____

_____

_____

_____

_____

MONTH #11 "Nothing can bring you peace but yourself." (Ralph Waldo Emerson)

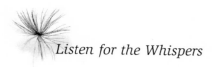

MONTH #12 "You cannot step twice in the same river, for other waters are continually flowing on." (Heraclitus)

Thankful Bouquets

My deepest gratitude goes to my publisher and new friend, Nan Wisherd. Her guidance, and her willingness to listen to and believe in *my* whispers, has made my commitment to helping others possible.

My message would not have been as clear without the skilled editing of Dean Lamanna. Thank you for your support and professional help.

A special thank you goes to Larry Verkeyn for his determination to find the perfect dandelion, thus creating the ideal book cover. You read my mind and made my idea come alive.

To Joy Ufema, a nationally known pioneer in the field of death and dying, thank you for the opportunity to share my story with you on a cool spring day at your farm. I am deeply grateful that you agreed to lend your voice and spirit to my work.

And thanks to Leslie Gilbert for capturing the true me with her camera.

Finally, in remembrance of my dear friend Melissa, who wisely gave me my first journal—that is where it all began.

About the Author

Born in upstate New York, Kim Kluxen Meredith's formal education at Washington College, the University of Madrid, and the Philadelphia Paralegal Institute prepared her well for her legal duties and high school lessons. But her most important life lessons resulted from her untimely widowhood and from the "whispers" that guided her from her grief.

Kim has called Lancaster, PA home since 1977 where today she is in her twenty-first year as an educator. She hopes to soon devote all of her time to writing, gardening, traveling, and to her children and grandchildren. Each summer Kim and her husband Tom look forward to collecting more memories with their growing families at the Jersey Shore.